The Insightful Leader

The Insightful Leader

Find Your Leadership Superpowers, Crush Limiting Beliefs, and Abolish Self-Sabotaging Behaviors

Carlann Fergusson

 PRAEGER™

An Imprint of ABC-CLIO, LLC

Santa Barbara, California • Denver, Colorado

Library of Congress Cataloging-in-Publication Data

Names: Fergusson, Carlann, author.
Title: The insightful leader : find your leadership superpowers, crush
   limiting beliefs, and abolish self-sabotaging behaviors / Carlann
   Fergusson.
Description: Santa Barbara, California : Praeger, [2018] | Includes
   bibliographical references and index.
Identifiers: LCCN 2018011053 (print) | LCCN 2018012753 (ebook) | ISBN
   9781440862816 (eBook) | ISBN 9781440862809 (hardcopy : alk. paper)
Subjects: LCSH: Leadership.
Classification: LCC HD57.7 (ebook) | LCC HD57.7 .F465 2018 (print) | DDC
   658.4/092—dc23
LC record available at https://lccn.loc.gov/2018011053

ISBN: 978-1-4408-6280-9 (print)
      978-1-4408-6281-6 (ebook)

22 21 20 19 18   1 2 3 4 5

This book is also available as an eBook.

Praeger
An Imprint of ABC-CLIO, LLC

ABC-CLIO, LLC
130 Cremona Drive, P.O. Box 1911
Santa Barbara, California 93116-1911
www.abc-clio.com

This book is printed on acid-free paper ∞

Manufactured in the United States of America

Contents

Introduction: That Nagging Feeling

When we are no longer able to change a situation, we are challenged
to change ourselves.
—Viktor Frankl, Austrian neurologist and psychiatrist and
Holocaust survivor

You are an experienced and successful leader. You have a solid foundation of
competencies for your leadership level. You've taken the leadership-development courses. You've read the books about the ten things great leaders do.
Maybe you've even gone back to college, but it still feels like something is
missing. You know you are capable of even greater leadership.

You push the thought aside and run off to the next meeting. You and
your team are getting results, and there is no indication that anyone
thinks you are less than competent. But the feeling is still there. Your
leadership is not quite where you want it to be; it's just not good enough.
Possibly you are subconsciously picking up on the body language of your
direct reports, peers, or boss. You replay interactions in your head. What
is causing this paranoia? You tell yourself it's your incredibly high standards, but, again, that deep knowing that there is something more to
learn is urging you to reach further.

Maybe your career is on fire, and you're being recognized as the next
successor to a key role in the company. You second-guess if you really
have what it takes to step into those bigger shoes. If only you felt a bit
more confident about having a larger group follow you into the future.

Maybe your climb up the leadership ladder has slowed. Perhaps you've
gone from being one of the favored individuals getting plum assignments
and making presentations to senior leaders to being one of the masses.
You watch curiously as others receive coveted assignments, present to the

executive staff, or attend a board of directors meeting. You look on in frustration as other seemingly less-accomplished leaders get put on the succession plan or get promoted.

Regardless of what is causing this feeling of missing something important, you want to figure it out and fill that void. This is when the brain tries to protect your self-image by rationalizing. In an effort to convince yourself that you are fine just the way you are, you compare yourself to leaders you believe to be less capable. You reminisce about accomplishments that prove your value to the company. You examine your last few performance reviews. This works for another few days, and then that nagging feeling returns. You wonder if perhaps you need to do more—try harder, work later, be more patient, be more optimistic. You are missing something, and you are determined to ascertain what it is. You muster up the courage to have a frank discussion with your boss. You ask for feedback, but you get a vague response.

What could be missing?

Nothing.

Nothing is missing. It's not that you need to follow some leadership recipe or do these ten things great leaders do or stop doing these three things poor leaders do. It's not that you need to schmooze your boss or other influential leaders. Nor is it that you need to attend yet another leadership course.

These factors aren't getting in the way of your success. Stop worrying that you aren't good enough or that something is missing. It is not that you are too little.

It's the opposite.

The problem is you are a bit too much.

A few key strengths have become too strong. Those hard-earned gifts that got you to this point in your life and career are getting in your way instead of taking you further. They are not only interfering with your leadership and your career but also standing in the way of your progress, your dreams, and your relationships. It's not that you need to find a way to turn off these strengths. They are some of your best qualities as a leader. They need to continue to shine; there are just times when they need to shine less brightly. There are times when the behaviors, outcomes, and energy these strengths create are not what you intended.

Perhaps you push your ideas a little too hard, share the cool stuff you know a bit too much, feel for others too deeply, critique a tad too often, or are a smidge too exacting. If you have a gnawing feeling that there is an even better leader within you, if your mind replays interactions with others that you know deep down could have gone better, or if you want to make certain that you get the career opportunities you desire, then this book is for you. It's not that you are missing some skill or experience that you need to acquire from some external source. Instead, the transformation will come from deeper self-awareness and insight that is gained by focusing internally. The message others are quietly sending is, "We don't need you to continue to grow; we need you to change."

This subtle message comes to every great leader at some point on the career path. It usually shows up when the last managerial level has been mastered and the leader is positioning to move up to the next rung on the leadership ladder. Once deciphered, this whispering is the wake-up call that propels strong leaders forward.

The process shared in *The Insightful Leader* is going to help you become the leader you imagine. It is going to help you remove the burden of second-guessing your interactions with others. The process came from coaching hundreds of leaders and noticing similar patterns. It was refined from being privy to thousands of leaders' performance, promotional, and succession-planning discussions. It grew from my own deep personal exploration and continued desire to be a better leader. It blossomed from leaving the executive ranks and helping leaders rise to greater positions of influence. Most of all, it was born from a passion for helping leaders transform into their incredible best selves to bring out the best in those who work with them.

The Insightful Leader will help you stop standing in the way of your own success. You will learn that the "something" that keeps you from advancing does not originate from your weaknesses but from your strengths—those phenomenal strengths that are your superpowers. You will discover that the unlikely source of these strengths stems from your earlier life challenges. These trials not only gave birth to these strengths but also gave you resilience and courage. These abilities allowed you to successfully maneuver through challenges so your leadership potential could be recognized. Unfortunately, the continued praise and recognition you received for these strengths created an overdependency on their use.

To discover your superpowers, you will be guided through a process to step aside from your biases and become the neutral observer. You will identify when their overuse causes unintended consequences to your leadership. *The Insightful Leader* will help you shift your perspective so you can challenge the outdated beliefs connected to your superpower's overuse. You will learn the precise actions needed to bring your superpower back into balance without eliminating the benefits it brings to your leadership and to your organization. In the final chapters, you'll gain the support tools necessary to eliminate negative perceptions and create lasting success.

Personal change is a rewarding discovery of who you are at your deepest level. You will come out of the process with renewed energy, purpose, and confidence to put your best authentic self forward. It is a quest focused on you that also has significant implications for others working with you. You will become a better leader and a better role model who creates a space where others are energized to work together.

Move through the book at your own pace. Give yourself time for deeper contemplation. Create space to try out new thoughts and behaviors.

Now that you know our purpose together, let's get started.

PART 1

Preparing for Insight

If you plan on being anything less than you are capable of being, you will probably be unhappy all the days of your life.

—Abraham Maslow, American psychologist

CHAPTER ONE

Rising from Adversity

When everything seems to be going against you, remember that the airplane takes off against the wind, not with it.
—Henry Ford, American business magnate
and founder of Ford Motor Company

Those incredible strengths that are the source of your leadership greatness and current frustration did not arise from education, training, or advantage. They came from an unlikely source—adversity. All leaders rise from adversity. No one gets into the ranks of leadership unscathed.

I'm not implying that there is an arduous hazing ritual for leaders. The difficult experience was often much earlier in the life of a leader, usually well before the individual considered becoming a leader. It was either an event or a series of events in the person's life. The exact nature of this adversity differs greatly from leader to leader. For some it can be easily identified, such as alcoholic parents, mental or physical abuse, severe bullying at school, physical trauma, living in a dangerous area, or the traumatic death of a loved one. For others, it is less evident, such as trying to be the mediator to fighting parents, attempting to meet the unreasonably high expectations of a well-meaning mentor, or listening wide-eyed to a grandfather's frequent retelling of his own life horrors. This past stressful experience triggered fear, but the courageous youngster discovered ways to fight back. They reframed the event from an attack to a challenge. They channeled their fear response into steadfast determination or fiery defiance. This future leader learned coping skills, developed survival behaviors, and gained resilience. Through repetition, these survival behaviors became more highly developed abilities. Later in life, they morphed into key leadership strengths—strengths not developed by those individuals who did not experience early adversity, strengths also not developed by those who viewed their early challenges as insurmountable and saw themselves as helpless victims of circumstance.

I've heard hundreds of leaders' stories of early adversity in my decades of coaching, and I'm always in awe of their courage and resilience. As youths, they demonstrated advanced problem solving and intelligence far beyond that expected for their age. Their cunningness at finding ways to limit their exposure to their persecutors and their ability to stay focused on a better tomorrow are testaments to their brilliance. The fact that they had become successful executives with a few rough edges rather than individuals blaming their pasts for career limitations is admirable. Their capacity to create rules to serve as mental constructs for survival in the most arduous of circumstances rather than fracture into depression, anxiety, or posttraumatic stress disorder is astonishing.

At first, most leaders don't recognize their extraordinary courage and resilience. They filed the event and their response into their subconscious as just another challenge that was important to their development. Some even have a difficult time recalling the adverse event. Not until they identify the superpower and the underlying survival belief can they recollect with clarity the initiating events. They understand that most people experience some type of adversity in their lives and they see theirs as no different. However, their response to adversity is different. These early leaders rejected their persecutors' attempts to cast them in the role of victim. Instead of focusing on what they couldn't do, they focused on what they could do. They found some way to gain control over the situation to lessen or alter the outcome. They focused on an immediate goal that gave them a sense of progress. Depending on the leader, the objective was achieving superior grades to garner approval, taking a job to avoid going home after school, serving as the target to prevent a little sister from being abused, or keeping their emotions steady so as not to add to the chaos. These tough-minded individuals gained an early edge on the leadership competencies of tenacity, perseverance, and goal setting.

It is not the severity of adversity but rather the individual's ability to rise from these situations that is essential to future success. Adults who continue to see themselves as victims of circumstance are not going to have the same ability to take control of future situations as adults who reframe past stressful events as being crucial to their development. These resilient individuals apply their fortitude and learned survival skills to other challenges in life and work. Early in their careers, this confidence to overcome obstacles is what got them noticed as potential leaders. It is also what continues to fuel their success—until those same survival skills that act as the source of their greatest leadership strengths become their biggest leadership weaknesses.

Leadership capability may first catch the attention of others in college, in the military, or in early employment, but the situations are similar. A group the future leader is a part of is challenged with a difficult task or objective. Having overcome early life challenges, the leader perceives this challenge as much less daunting than others on the team. After all, he has overcome much worse. While his colleagues worry about how to approach the challenge or are immobilized and completely overwhelmed, the future leader's brain is on task. This resilient individual is already sorting through the known and unknown, processing possible solutions, and creating a likely plan of action. When this individual speaks up, saying he has ideas on how to handle the situation, the rest of the team breathes a sigh of relief. They eagerly follow their now designated leader.

To guide the group to success, the individual calls upon the skills learned through his past adverse experience. Perhaps it was an ability to quickly see potential negative consequences or to see the desired outcome and figure out the steps needed to get there. Maybe it was the ability to quickly flex to changing circumstances or to anticipate the responses of others. Whatever well-practiced strengths are deployed, the individual takes charge, and the team applauds his leadership capabilities and courage. Later, the individual is promoted into management for demonstrating advanced thinking and skills.

Since leadership consists of overcoming multiple challenges, the leader is asked to rise to a challenge again and again. As the leader succeeds, he is again reinforced. His skills and beliefs of what creates success are once again strengthened. Then the leader gets the ultimate reinforcement by being promoted to the next level. Now he believes that this ability is his superpower. Just like the superheroes Iron Man, Storm, Batman, Wonder Woman, or Black Panther, the leader relies on this superpower to save the day.

If he gets in a bind, he whips this strength out.

If the company needs to solve a difficult dilemma, she offers to lend her power to the cause.

If he wants to add value to a new team, he demonstrates this gift.

Soon, everyone in the company knows to contact this leader when you need his or her specific strength.

For a while this recognition continues. Then, as the leader continues to increase his use of this same strength, he becomes aware that he is no longer garnering positive attention. Perhaps it is a nagging feeling. Perhaps the leader notices he is less and less sought out for assistance. Maybe he is not being offered the highly visible projects or is being passed over for promotions. Confused, the leader is unaware that the previous reinforcement unintentionally strengthened his already strong skills and beliefs until they became too strong. Suddenly, the talk behind closed doors in performance discussions and succession planning is focused on the negative impact of this leader's overused strengths.

Picture Marvel's superhero, the Hulk. The Hulk has a wonderful gift of muscular strength. He can remove heavy physical barriers. With a sweep of his arms, he can knock away vehicles and obstacles to clear a path for his team of Avengers. The perception is that he is extremely helpful . . . until his strength becomes too strong.

When his behavior is overamplified, he leaves a path of destruction. He becomes scary—someone to avoid. Even his caring team has to gently but forcefully persuade him to reel his powers back in.

Unfortunately, the same thing happens to a leader's superpowers.

When constant success reinforces strengths, leaders lose sight of the unintended consequences of allowing their strengths to get too strong. Leaders exceptionally good at figuring out the details of projects are now perceived as nitpickers and pessimists. Leaders who make the tough decisions and stay in their analytical minds, refusing to allow feelings to cloud their judgment, are seen as cold and uncaring. Intellectually curious people who love to research and bring new approaches to the work start sharing too much of their knowledge in meetings and get labeled as know-it-alls. These once-effective responses are no longer having the effect the leaders desire. The superpowers have gotten out of their control.

When I was in my twenties, I worked for the U.S. government's Bureau of Engraving and Printing. I was the up-and-coming fair-haired manager. My performance reviews were outstanding. I was asked to be on every special project and served on congressional task forces. I wrote the speeches for the head of our agency. I was on the fast track to success. My strengths were heavily reinforced. I was considered highly results oriented, tenacious, visionary, and highly analytic—all desired abilities for leadership. There didn't seem to be any limit to my future.

I was thrilled but not surprised when I was invited by my boss to apply for a governmentwide leadership-development program. It was an opportunity to represent not only the bureau but also the Treasury Department. I accepted the challenge. After the second phase of interviews, I received notice that I was included among the final candidates. Feeling confident, I waited impatiently for the verdict. After what seemed an eternity, my boss finally called me into his office. I looked at him with excited anticipation. He told me, "Carlann, you should feel very proud to have made it as a finalist, but you were not selected."

My heart sank. I couldn't believe it. I had been one of the most favored managers at the bureau, always getting the opportunities. How could this be? It didn't make sense. I needed to know why, so I asked.

My boss responded as if he'd rehearsed his response: "The other finalists had more experience." I heard the statement, but it didn't feel right. My boss's body language was telling me he was hiding something. I pressed for more details but got nothing. I left my boss's office bewildered.

I asked my function's vice president but received the same story. Deciding the truth was more important than denying there was a problem, I mustered the courage to ask the head of our agency for feedback. Having worked closely with him as his speechwriter, I hoped he would be candid.

He was.

He replied, "Carlann, I'm not sure what is causing this, but you are seen as unfriendly. I don't experience you this way, but others do."

As I recall this memory, I am transported back in time. I stand there shocked for what seems like an eternity instead of the few seconds that actually tick by. In that quick pace of the clock's second hand, my brain chatter is defiantly reeling.

"I'm *not* unfriendly. I have friends. How dare he say I'm unfriendly! This is ridiculous. It must be that the person selected was better at sucking up to the executive staff. How in the world did they come up with 'unfriendly' from my responses in the interviews? This is ridiculous!"

My brain quickly enters a choice point—fight back or run. Luckily, my brain recognizes that this CEO has more positional power and yells, "Run!"

I stand wide-eyed and utter quietly, "Thank you for the feedback. I'll give this some serious thought." I shoot out the door and race-walk back to my office with elbows pumping. My defensive brain goes back to its squirrel-like chatter, telling me I can't be the source of the problem.

Ironically, I was hoping someone would give me honest feedback, and when someone finally has the courage to tell me the candid, honest reason discussed behind the closed doors of the selection committee, my survival brain wants to bite the person's head off. My brain is working hard to protect my self-image of being a friendly leader.

I go home, vent to my husband, and process through the anger. I state my case to him that I have friends. I offer the brilliant argument that managers can't be friends with their employees because it limits their ability to make the tough calls. I justify my position for over ten minutes. Then, once the flight-or-fight adrenaline wears off, I am quiet.

After a few deep breaths, my brain resurfaces the subconscious nudging that something about what the head of our agency said is true. My subconscious knows that my previous argument was off topic—it's not about being friends; it's about being friendly. The subconscious pokes me again. Whether I like it or not, there is truth in the statement. I am unfriendly.

But I don't want to be seen as unfriendly. I want to be seen as friendly. I don't want to be seen as a dictatorial leader. I want to be seen as approachable.

It's my intention to be friendly, but let's face it; my intention doesn't matter. I can argue for years about my intention, but it won't change the perception. The perception is that I am unfriendly.

I am unfriendly.

I take a deep breath and say it again.

I am unfriendly.

I let that soak in. Crap.

Here comes the disappointment, but now I'm aware it is disappointment in myself. I could spend time feeling sorry for myself, but I'm too analytical for that. My brain has been trained to find the root cause. I start to dig.

What am I doing that could create the perception in others that I am unfriendly?

My subconscious chimes in, "You are so task oriented that you dive right into assignments. You don't ask people how they are doing. Heck, you hardly say 'hello.' Instead, you start conversations with 'Tell me where we are with this project' or 'I've got a new project for you.' You portray that you're all logic and process focused."

It feels a bit like I'm off-balance. I thought my results orientation, highly analytic mind, and ability to see the future and find the right path to reach it were qualities that got me promoted. I'm aware that these strengths can be my greatest attributes, but the feedback makes me mindful of how they are also a source of frustration to others. It is clear that there are unintended consequences of overusing these strengths.

Double crap.

I have to own it—I am unfriendly. Not all the time, but there are plenty of times I am unfriendly. Forget trying to protect my self-concept of being this effective, efficient, and approachable leader. Like the Hulk, my superpowers are on overdrive, and I'm leaving a path of destruction.

If you asked me back then what the event was that triggered this superpower, I would have said very stoically that I learned it from my dad, a man who was extremely task oriented and showed little emotion.

Nice response, but I'm nowhere close to the real answer. Plus, I can't pinpoint it to one event. My statement is a generalization.

If, instead, you asked me to tell you about the first event that pops into my mind when I think of a time when it was critical to my safety to withhold any emotion—when it was a matter of survival—my response is totally different. My stomach tightens up, my breathing gets shallow, and my underarms sweat as an image immediately appears in my brain.

I'm six, and my sister is eight. We are at the dinner table that we have set for the big Sunday meal. We are in our dresses with napkins and hands folded in our laps—the perfect picture of ladylike etiquette. Then my sister blurts out that she doesn't like the brussels sprouts. Not thinking of the consequences, I agree. A familiar red flush creeps up my father's neck. His eyes become narrow, and his pupils contract into beady dots of pure black. My dad enters full-on rage mode. He's screaming at the top of his lungs about how ungrateful we are, how lazy we are, and how hard he works. The hatred in his eyes is piercing through me. I start to cry. He continues to scream criticisms at me, but I can't hear him anymore because I'm crying so hard my throat is clenching around my recently swallowed food. I'm taking in gulps of breath. He interprets my crying as a sign of weakness, and this brings forth a new tyranny of fury. The energy feels as if an out-of-control freight train is heading straight for me. He yells at me to stop crying. He bellows about how ugly I am when I cry, and he screams for me to suck it up and stop feeling sorry for myself. I look to my mother for support, but she has already numbed herself for the night with her usual two gin martinis before dinner. She now hides behind her glass of wine as if she is trying to make herself smaller. She has learned that if she intervenes, it will just make matters worse. I know I'm on my own. I choke back my tears and try to swallow my emotions down as far as they will go. I summon a mantra of "Don't show any emotions! Don't show any emotions!" It begins to work. I suppress the tears and shift my sadness to defiance. I stare at him coolly. His anger subsides. We finish dinner in silence. The rest of the evening continues as if nothing has happened.

The next weekend my sister and I are riding our bikes. My dad shows up with his camera to take a photo. In his mind, he is the famous photographer Ansel Adams, and this is a major photo shoot. Any misplaced hair or misaligned blouse is a reminder that his subject is not cooperating. As usual, I have dirt on my knees. This sets off another of his rage attacks.

He starts screaming a list of my shortcomings—that I'm clumsy and unladylike and that I purposely try to make him look bad. My eyes start to fill with tears, but then I remember my mantra: "Don't show your feelings. You'll only make it worse." I pull back my shoulders, raise my head, and look at him with steadfastness. I don't break. It works! I produce a smile of contempt that screams, "I hate you!" He takes the photo and leaves satisfied.

This survival skill is now set. The sensitive, empathic child who would cry over a dead bunny in the road is gone. The message is clear: "Don't show your emotions. Stay in your analytic brain."

Even recounting this memory raises all the emotions of the event, and my chest feels constricted. In this moment, there is no mature understanding that his mental challenges made him incapable of empathy; there is only the immediate reliving of the event, and this is powerful. The insights are lightning bolts of realization.

Upon hearing my original description of the reason for the unfriendly behavior, you might have thought, "Oh, her dad didn't show emotion, so it was a role-model thing—case closed." As a coach, you might help me acknowledge that my dad was not a great role model. However, this conclusion only scratches the surface. It's not what made me rise from adversity. It's not what gave me my incredible strengths that got me noticed. Not only that, but my statement of logic wasn't even correct. I essentially said, "My dad didn't show any emotion." That's totally incorrect. A rage attack is an explosion of emotion. The true statement is that he was very adept at showing his unbridled emotion. The reality is that he was incapable of empathizing with others. He was certainly a taskmaster and a poor role model, but he did show his emotions.

It is important for me to acknowledge my adversity. Only by reliving this as an adult can I see the leadership qualities it gave me. Only then can I be thankful for the survival skills that helped me navigate a dysfunctional childhood.

Decades ago, when I worked through my leadership problem of being highly analytic and unfriendly, I didn't know how to uncover the source of this career limiter. Instead, I made a conscious effort to try to be friendlier. For the next several weeks, I slowed myself down and spent time asking my employees about their kids, their weekends, and their commutes. I put placeholders in my calendar at the end of each project to celebrate accomplishments. I smiled more. I chatted more. But deep inside I still felt like I was wasting time trying to be friendly. While I asked about my colleagues' kids, my brain chatter reminded me about all the things I needed to get done. I hardly heard their responses. I did want to be friendlier, but my core beliefs had not changed; I was only going through the motions.

When the next big project came with an impossibly short deadline, the old behaviors popped right back out. I backslid into the demanding taskmaster. My team responded to the change in behavior by shooting glances at each other that screamed, "Here we go again." This was my wake-up call that I had not challenged the underlying beliefs standing in the way of my success. Not until I figured out why I believed that making the effort to build relationships was a waste of time was I going to change. Not until I challenged my belief that showing feelings was a sign of weakness was I going to become a better leader. To become an insightful leader, I discovered that I needed to (1) find my superpower, (2) identify my adversity, and (3) challenge my beliefs.

Maybe you can relate to my story in several ways. Perhaps, however, you are thinking that overused superpowers only happen early in your leadership career and that you couldn't possibly be prone to this because you are an accomplished, seasoned executive.

Think again.

All leaders go through a point in their careers when they receive tough feedback alluding to an overused strength. Those wonderful abilities that enabled you to rise from adversity will get to a point where they become overused and affect your career, effectiveness, and happiness. The initial awareness can come early in your career, or it may come after numerous promotions have supercharged the strength. It can happen when you are in your twenties, but it can also happen in your thirties, forties, or fifties. The earlier you find out about your overused superpower, the easier it is to correct because it has not had extra decades of reinforcement.

Not even great leaders are immune. I worked for Intel for twelve years when Andy Grove was the president and CEO. He was Jewish and grew up in Nazi-occupied Budapest, Hungary. When he was young, his father was arrested and sent to a labor camp. He and his mother took on false identities to hide. Having survived the German siege of Budapest, Andy grew up in Communist-controlled Hungary, where many young people were killed and others interned. At the age of twenty, he took a major risk and escaped across the border into Austria. At an Intel leadership retreat, Andy spoke of crawling on his belly across the fields while bullets whizzed over his head. He saw many other escapees shot and killed. He was constantly looking over his shoulder to see if anyone was after him but remained determined to make it across to Austria.

Not surprisingly, Andy became a leader great at scanning the environment for what was coming next. He referred to this as seeing the "next inflection point" and held his entire team of leaders at Intel responsible for monitoring and planning for not only the next great evolution of a product but also the next revolution of something entirely new. He continued to be a strong strategist and risk taker.

When I started with Intel, there was an abundance mentality. There was more than enough opportunity for all players, and we did not fret about the other companies in the microprocessor world. We kept our eyes on the horizon, and the company flourished. Later, though, there was a shift. Andy, who had grown up scanning his environment for opportunities while also looking over his shoulder for danger, became focused on our competition. He was worried they would not only catch up to us but also surpass us. It was becoming more difficult to discern the next great thing, and Andy changed his focus from wonderful possibilities to fear of the enemy. We shifted to a scarcity mind-set. There was now a limited piece of the pie, and we needed to make sure we owned it. During this shift, Andy wrote the book *Only the Paranoid Survive*.[1] He described inflection points and his shift in view: "Business success contains the seeds of its own destruction. The more successful you are, the more people want a chunk of your business and then another chunk and then another until there is nothing."

Intel's advantage as the "we can do anything" company waned as Andy focused on fear. His leaders became risk-averse and scared to make decisions. During this time, I used to say to my peers, "Never have I worked so hard to get so little done." Every plan for change was scrutinized and questioned. We spent months documenting every possible outcome and creating countless contingency plans. Those focused on the next great product became filled with anxiousness rather than possibility. As we looked over our shoulder, we missed the dawn of a new horizon. Our products became commodities. To position the company to compete on price, we began eliminating jobs and employees. I knew we had become too fat, but one massive layoff was followed by another and then another. Those remaining were burdened with unmanageable workloads and waited in fear of the next downsizing. We adopted our leader's adversity-learned survival skill of looking over our shoulders.

That great skill of scanning the environment shifted from scanning for opportunities to scanning relentlessly for signs of the enemy. It wasn't that Andy wasn't a great leader; he was. It's just that his strength became

---

1. Andrew S. Grove, *Only the Paranoid Survive: How to Exploit the Crisis Points That Challenge Every Company*, New York: Doubleday, 1996.

overamplified. His continued reinforcement of this strength turned it into a superpower that had unintended consequences.

No leader intentionally overuses strengths and creates negative perceptions. No leader wants to be the person who is unfriendly or paranoid or who leaves casualties. Becoming a better leader requires gaining insight into who you really are. It requires change at the core of your beliefs. It requires challenging your go-to behaviors when things get tough. It requires toning down what you consider to be your best traits and abilities.

There are three steps to becoming an insightful leader:

1. Find your superpower.
2. Identify your adversity.
3. Challenge your beliefs.

Part II of this book will help you find your amazing superpower and the unintended consequences it can create. You will recognize its gifts and where it might cause you to be perceived as egotistical or manipulative. You'll get recommendations to start using right away to bring your strengths back into balance.

Part III will help you identify the adversity that developed your superpowers. It will explain why certain individuals or circumstances trigger your overuse and how that results in you acting in a less-than-constructive manner. Part III will also challenge those deeply held survival beliefs that fuel your superpower overuse. You'll be able to acknowledge these beliefs for helping you to overcome your adversity and then replace them with beliefs that better fit your current experiences. This will lead to lasting change and allow you to become the leader you know you are capable of being.

Your brain may already be exploring what strengths you received and their possible negative outcomes if overused. However, before you jump into step one of discovering your superpowers, you'll need to turn off that natural defensive chatter in your mind so that you can fully challenge your thinking. This will also help you step aside from your point of view and see things clearly from other people's perspective.

CHAPTER TWO

Discovering Your Superpowers

Whatever we refuse to recognize about ourselves has a way of rearing its head and making itself known when we least expect it.
—Debbie Ford,
American author, *The Dark Side of the Light Chasers*

Not until you see the impact through the eyes of others can you understand how your strongest strengths become your biggest weaknesses. This shift in perspective requires you to keep your mind open and observe your body's response as you read through the descriptions of the superpowers. These ten superpower behaviors are quite similar among talented leaders, even though the adversity, challenges, and reinforcing experiences that created your superpowers are unique to you. Understanding these most commonly overused strengths will not only enable you to find your superpowers but also better understand the source of your frustration with other leaders' behaviors.

These ten superpowers evolved from researching the shared symptoms of derailed executives and then looking deeper for the source of these perceptions. As part of my leadership role within corporations, I observed thousands of conversations regarding promotions, succession planning, performance reviews, demotions, and terminations. This work gave me plenty of opportunities to notice the patterns and ask deeper questions to determine what stalled a promising leader while another was selected for career opportunities. The patterns started to emerge. I noticed these same superpowers were also the most common themes of criticism in 360-degree feedback to leaders. They became a great tool for helping executives decipher what their bosses, peers, and direct reports were trying to tell them. Once I formally began creating the list, I validated it with numerous executive teams at different companies and then took it on the road, speaking to groups of two hundred to five hundred leaders at conferences. The list of superpowers and their unintended negative attributes resonated with audiences. They were surprised to learn that the same abilities and behaviors their companies had reinforced in them through career-advancement opportunities or promotions eventually came to limit their careers.

The Ten Superpowers

The Overused Strength		The Unintended Negative Perception	
1.	Results Driven	A.	Impractical
2.	Problem Finder	B.	Pessimistic
3.	Intellectually Curious	C.	Know-It-All
4.	Empathic	D.	Needy
5.	Visionary	E.	Demanding
6.	Highly Analytic	F.	Uncaring
7.	Humble	G.	Condescending
8.	Precise	H.	Rigid
9.	Great Listener	I.	Lacking Confidence
10.	Calm under Pressure	J.	Apathetic

In order to create lasting behavioral change, you need to look objectively at your superpowers, understand others' perspectives, revisit a time of adversity, challenge your beliefs, and risk trying new behaviors. Before you start on these steps, it is important to eliminate your personal protection device: the defensive brain. To do this, you'll need to take on the role of the neutral observer. This isn't easy. The brain's natural defenses want to preserve your sense of self. It can be difficult to hold up the mirror and really stare at the reflection and make observations instead of judgments. It requires you to step aside from your own needs, perspectives, and experiences and to challenge your assumptions. These deeply held conventions about what is best for your continued existence have been around a long time and were essential not only to your early success but also to your entry into leadership. Without challenging your thoughts, you will continue to think that these beliefs guarantee future success.

Your Defensive Mind

The brain is an incredible piece of machinery structured not only to help us learn but also to help us survive. You need to understand this wiring for survival at a deeper level because it creates defenses that can keep you from becoming more cognizant of your overused strengths and the perspectives they create. It also keeps painful subconscious truths hidden from your awareness and tells you to justify who you are rather than allow you to become the leader you want to be.

Here is the great news: your defensiveness is all in your mind. Here is the bad news: your brain is very good at protecting you.

To avoid turning this into a book about the brain, I'm going to give an oversimplified view of the brain's processing. It will be just enough information to identify the triggers to your natural defenses but not so much that I leave you swirling in your synapses and contemplating the meaning of life.

Although your brain acts as one unit, it has areas dedicated to specific functions. Your brain is capable of both instinctual responses designed for our continual survival and advanced reasoning functions that can include problem solving, reasoning, empathy, and compassion. The higher functions of your brain enable you to take feedback and examine it to determine what aspects could be true. This calm, intellectual functioning provides the emotional maturity necessary to seek out criticism, reflect on your behavior, and recognize that you are not perfect. Such advanced reasoning allows you to accept that you need to change. It also helps you to select which new behaviors to try and to evaluate their effectiveness.

With this higher thinking, you have the capacity to be an enlightened individual who always looks at things from different perspectives. You can be in touch with the needs of others, understand your own needs, and calmly go about your days. It is a wonderful feeling, but for the majority of individuals who have not been able to escape the daily stressors of life, it doesn't last.

The reason this mature response is short-lived is because the survival parts of your brain, located closer to the brain stem, are so great at protecting you from danger and driving you toward success that they override your more advanced thinking processes. This midbrain developed earlier than the higher-functioning areas of the brain. The survival functions of your brain focus on one simple outcome: keep this body alive. They do this by prioritizing two objectives: avoid pain and attain pleasure. The midbrain is constantly processing what is safe or unsafe, pleasurable or painful, right or wrong. It also stores your reactions as information for future use. Whatever kept you safe or brought you pleasure is stored as an effective response. Whatever did not work, left you in a negative situation, or did not help you achieve your desired outcome is stored as something not worth repeating. These past experiences and emotions create memories and unconscious value judgments. This connection is especially true if the behavior's origins were connected to fear—the strongest emotion. Fear is your brain's way of alerting you to a potentially unsafe situation. When fear occurs, it shuts down your higher-functioning brain and focuses everything on survival.

These instinctual parts of the midbrain act as your personal squirrel, alerting you to danger by chirping out shrill warning cries and shaking its tail intensely. When you interpret something as being potentially life threatening, your flight-or-fight response is triggered. The flight-or-fight response prepares the body to either run away from the danger or attack the threat. It dumps adrenaline and noradrenaline hormones, sending signals to shorten the breath, tense the muscles, dilate the pupils, and send blood to the extremities. These hormones prepare your body for one of two choices: run like a scared deer or stand your ground and release a physical attack accompanied by threatening, angry screams. If you perceive that you are in a life-threatening situation, the flight-or-fight response will go on heightened alert, and you may even experience a sense of time decelerating and of choosing your actions in slow motion. Although you would swear you have entered a time warp, neuroscience has proven this phenomenon is your brain increasing its speed and ability to receive and process massive amounts of data in order to make split-second decisions.

This flight-or-fight response is extremely helpful for fighting off the threats of lions and bears. It is also helpful for running away or standing your ground when dealing with a bully or someone physically attacking you. Even when you are at a disadvantage, such as being a child with an adult attacker, it provides a heightened alertness that allows you to take in information that could be helpful to avoiding a future attack (e.g., observing the nuances of a person's mood changing so that you can make yourself absent in the future when you see similar changes in the individual).

The thorny problem is that most adults rarely encounter the threats your brain was designed to protect you against. You are rarely, and hopefully never, attacked by a lion, challenged by a grizzly, or held at gunpoint by another human. Therefore, your flight-or-fight response has expanded from protecting you from physical danger to protecting you from psychological danger. This response is triggered when any situation raises emotions connected to worry, fear, anxiety, anger, or frustration. When given an especially challenging task to complete, this part of the brain will sort through your past experiences to select the actions and responses it believes have the highest probability of success. It also gets triggered to protect your ego, self-concept, dignity, and deeply held beliefs. These almost Neanderthal brain areas can take over at some of the most inopportune times, triggering the flight-or-fight response when someone calls you incompetent, overly sensitive, a drama queen, or an arrogant buffoon.

In fact, you can focus on this part of your brain right now by reliving a memory. Think back to a moment when someone at work gave you some very hurtful, unsolicited feedback. You were shocked such a thing was said about you. As soon as the words registered in your brain, anger swelled up in you.

Relive that memory for a moment. See yourself back in that situation. Remember what was happening, who was around, and the objects in the room. Now remember what was said.

Do you feel your chest tightening? Do you feel your breath getting shorter? Can you feel your pulse quickening? Are your muscles tightening? Are your teeth clenching?

Welcome to your instinctive brain and the flight-or-fight response. Your brain perceives an attack—a threat to your existence. But there is no knife-wielding person in front of you. There is no monster baring saber teeth, growling, and ready to pounce. Your brain doesn't care. It is protecting you from an attack—a *psychological* attack. It is sheltering you from pain. The discomfort it is avoiding is an attack on your self-concept. Your survival brain is keeping you from the wound of knowing that the self-image you want to project to others is not what others are experiencing. So instead of calmly observing the situation, you are now primed and pumped to run like a mad person through the corporate jungle to escape the predator giving you feedback or to pummel the person with a barrage of verbal counterattacks.

When your squirrel brain sends the shrill warning chirp, it gives you two immediate choices: run or attack. You can escape by nodding in fake agreement, giving the other person some trumped-up excuse as to why you have to leave, and getting out as fast as you can. Or you can fight back and release the built-up energy by yelling back at the person, defending your self-concept, and agitatedly rattling off why this statement is not true.

Later, in a matter of minutes or hours, your subconscious might kick in with an awareness that there is some truth in what the other person told you. You now feel hurt and disappointed. These are those slumped-shoulder, pit-in-the-belly feelings. But the anger is often still there, so you may lash out at the person who gave you the feedback, countering with hurtful comments thrown like daggers at the other person. "How dare you hurt me like that? I thought better of you."

If the other person is in a higher position of power, you don't say it out loud; instead, you rattle off the statements in your mind chatter. "How dare he say that to me? Who does he think he is? I thought he was better than that. I thought he respected me."

You have just projected your deficiencies onto the other person. You are actually hurt and disappointed in yourself. You are trying to deal with the subconscious alerting you to a hidden truth—a truth you don't really care to deal with because it will require dealing with the pain of some-thing you have pushed down and away from who you believe you are today. Getting stuck in this natural defense is what keeps leaders from becoming more insightful. The good news is that you can challenge that annoying squirrel.

Staying Out of Your Defensive Mind

In the next chapter, you will uncover your superpowers and their unintended negative consequences. You will want to keep your midbrain from taking over and shutting down your higher-thinking brain. Follow-ing are three ways to keep your brain's squirrel chatter from detouring your discovery.

Your Body Doesn't Lie

The beliefs that serve as the foundation to these superpowers lie in your deeper unconscious mind. They were programmed many years ago to keep you safe and pain-free. Therefore, you could read a description of a superpower, and your defensive brain could keep you from recognizing that this is your heightened ability. You may quickly think of other lead-ers who exhibit this exaggerated strength, but you just can't fathom it is you. You may be completely unaware that your survival brain has just hijacked your higher-thinking functions and is throwing other leaders' names at you to protect your self-image. Therefore, you need some other tool to know when these defenses are at play.

Remember that flight-or-fight response?

Remember those feelings you conjured up with just the memory of someone giving you feedback you were not ready for?

Those physical responses are your trick for determining when you need to shift from thinking of other people who might possess this overused superpower to looking at yourself. When you have that flight-or-fight response, it is your body telling you your brain has gone into survival mode and is protecting your self-concept from acknowledging that you could possess the potentially destructive aspects of the superpower.

If the superpower description elicits no flight-or-fight response, and you do not try to place the label onto someone else, then it is not one of your descriptors. You already recognize in your higher-thinking state that there are *times* when each of us can be irresponsible, demanding, self-centered, manipulative, temperamental, helpless, or whatever negative overuse label is being portrayed.

However, if while you are reading a superpower description you feel your pulse quickening, your breaths getting shorter, your muscles tightening, a pit in your stomach, sweaty palms or underarms, a flush in your face, neck, or ears—*listen* to your body. It is trying to tell you that your survival brain has decided that the information is too painful and does not fit with your view of who you are.

As soon as you feel the flight-or-fight response percolating up your body, stop reading and *breathe.*

Take a long deep breath through your nose. Hold it for a few seconds, and then slowly let it out. Repeat this process at least three times.

This isn't some new-age advice. When you inhale fully, you are telling your instinctual brain that there is no threat—either physical or psychological. You are telling your survival brain that everything is okay and that it can switch functions back up to your rational, empathic, problem-solving mind. If you can breathe deeply, your brain knows you are not being attacked, not in crisis, and not in a fear state. It will stop the rush of hormones and allow you to access your frontal lobe.

If you start connecting other peoples' names to the descriptions and case testimonials, *stop* and continue to ask if this could be you. This redirection does not contradict your hypothesis that the person you identified possesses this characteristic. However, this book and these processes are for you and you alone.

Intention Does Not Always Equal Perception

An individual chooses her words and behavior based on a desired outcome, but often the expected outcome does not crystallize. In the example I gave of being seen as "unfriendly," I knew my intention was to be an approachable leader. I wanted to be tough but caring. I wanted to be someone people felt confident following. I would tell people I had an open-door policy and they could engage me at any time. When I chose my behavior to ask others about the status of their projects, I did not think it differed from my intention as a leader. Once I received the feedback of being seen as unfriendly, I became aware that others' perceptions of me did not align to my intention. They did not perceive me to be approachable. Please note I said "perceive." Seeing me as unfriendly is the other person's interpretation of my behavior or action. This outcome is not what I intended to create.

My brain's defensive chatter when receiving the feedback was proof I had fallen into the trap of thinking my intended outcome of being an approachable leader would be the same as others' perception of my leadership. My desire to argue that I was indeed friendly was just my brain's way of protecting my self-image. It was not taking into consideration their experience of my leadership.

There is no point in arguing about intention, even if our defensive brain is clamoring for justice. Only you know your original objective. Other people can't read your mind to check if this intention you are defending was actually your initial plan or if you are fabricating an excuse to defend your actions. They only know what they experienced when they encountered your behaviors. To those individuals, their interpretation of the situation is tangible fact. To you, your intention is tangible fact. Your intention and their perception are both right, and both are based in fact. Now you can see why a strong defense of your intention is pointless.

To improve your leadership, it is better to step aside from your own view and assume theirs. Intention doesn't always equal perception. Your desired outcome and other people's experience of that outcome are two different things. This one concept is a tremendous help with uncovering your superpowers and the negative perceptions their overuse might create. Keep your mind open by saying to yourself, "This is how this strength, if overused, can be perceived by others—it is not my intention." This thought will help you stay in the higher-functioning parts of the brain instead of drifting into the defensive survival brain. It will keep you open to exploring different superpowers so you can reveal yours.

As you read through the superpowers, place a star next to those that trigger your defensive mind. This will help you identify the superpower to pay extra attention to as you read the more thorough descriptions. The negative descriptors are intentionally judgments because this is how others describe the undesirable impact. Remember, it is only perception, not your intention. Just mark the observation and continue with your discovery.

Ask "What?" Instead of "Why?"

Once you recognize that a superpower is yours, you can examine the descriptor with childlike curiosity. Ask yourself, "What could I be doing that could create the negative perception?"

Avoid asking yourself, "Why do I do this?" "Why?" asks you to defend yourself, and this will just get your survival brain reengaged. Keep that pesky part of the brain out of your self-discovery.

Asking "What?" tells your brain that you already acknowledge the descriptor of the superpower as yours, and now you want to explore it further. It sends a signal that there is no need to engage your mind chatter in defense. It opens you up to exploration.

Getting through Years of Defense

The earlier in your career you discover your superpowers, the easier it is to avoid potentially destructive behaviors. The longer people continue to use and rely on the strength of a superpower, the more they believe it is critical to their success and the less likely they are to notice the fallout from its overuse.

Many times I've given feedback on these superpower issues to executives, and they've been shocked that something they saw as their special attribute could be perceived as anything but beneficial to the company.

"I thought my strong rational thought was one of my good traits."

"It is . . . when it is used in moderation. When it becomes too strong, you are perceived as lacking empathy. When it is viewed as inappropriate for an emotionally sensitive situation, others label you as a bully."

"But I've been this way for twenty years!"

Now we are dealing with twenty years of this leader believing he was promoted and reinforced for this ability that has become too strong. The defenses around the superpower behaviors are going to be deeply entrenched.

If this is the case for you, just be aware that you will need to listen carefully to your physical responses and any defensive mind chatter to pinpoint potential superpower issues. Keep asking yourself if you have heard any feedback in the past that might be interpreted as the intensified superpower. Remember the vague "unfriendly" feedback I received? What my CEO was really trying to tell me was that my superpower of being highly analytical was perceived as lacking empathy—not an exact match for uncovering my superpower and its impact, but close enough. Think back on your performance reviews and any 360-degree feedback or informal career discussions as you read the superpowers. Ask yourself if any of that feedback might be related to one of the negative outcomes of your superpower description.

Don't overlook feedback from your home life. Our overused superpowers don't just show up at work. We take them home, too. Overly task focused at work equals overly task focused at home. Problem finder at work equals critical parent at home.

More Than One Superpower

I received feedback on my first overused superpower of being overly task oriented when I was a manager. Looking back, I'm sure it had been overamplified for several years, but no one who worked for me was courageous enough to tell me directly. I'm sure they hinted at it, but I didn't get the hint. It wasn't until I was passed over for the high-potential program that I finally learned the truth.

Decades later, as a global senior director, I experienced a similar event with a different superpower. I was overseeing strategic planning and large-scale change management. I was extremely talented at helping leaders create a vision—even those leaders who thought they weren't visionary. Because the companies I worked for greatly appreciated these gifts of vision, the executives I worked with were hesitant to tell me about the behavioral impact of another overused strength. I knew they discussed behavioral perceptions in those closed-door succession-planning meetings, but it wasn't until much later that I learned what they were saying about me.

Our executive team was focusing on the legal and financial tasks of a major acquisition. I needed them to schedule time to plan for the impending merger of the acquired employees into our company and culture. I could clearly foresee the problems we were going to encounter if we didn't address how these employees would be integrated. I wasn't convincing the executive team to commit to any action, so I kept talking about the risks associated with delaying the multitude of actions needing completion. The transition date was looming precariously close. I kept bringing up the subject in operational and project meetings. I tried one-on-one meetings with the key executive players. Everywhere I went, I kept repeating myself louder and with more force.

Finally, the clearly exasperated CEO said, "Carlann, sometimes you push too hard. You are right that we need to prepare, but we have too many other priorities right now, and you aren't hearing that. Pushing us harder is not helpful. I know we won't be as prepared as you would like for the integration, but if we don't get the legal and financial requirements addressed, this will be a worse omission."

I think my mouth actually dropped open in shock and recognition that he was right. I was so focused on my crystal-clear vision of what was needed to reach our future that I was oblivious to the immediate demands on the executives. My too-clear vision of what we needed to do and cries of risks were like a whiny child asking for a drink of water while the parent is on an urgent phone call. The parent tries to motion to the child to stop, but this attempt is not heeded. Soon the child is screaming at the top of her lungs, and the parent, exasperated, yells, "Just STOP!" The kid is shocked into silence. It's not that the water wasn't needed; it just wasn't the right time. We would expect the lack of awareness and the escalation from a child but not from an adult. I'm sure the exasperated leaders in my situation were thinking, "This leader isn't taking an executive perspective."

Now you can see why it is so important to provide opportunities for leaders to uncover these superpower issues for themselves. Superpower issues can change over time, allowing a new issue to rear its ugly head as you gain experience and success. It's better for everyone to encounter the sting of embarrassment as you uncover your own potential career stallers than to wait until it's so egregious that someone is forced to tell you, or worse yet, you are pushed out of the organization and never told the real reason.

Don't Skip

Read each superpower description even if you get the urge to jump over one that you are certain is not yours. In the chapter title, I've only used one word to define the strength and one word to describe the negative impact of the overuse, so you may not readily see one that aligns exactly to the feedback you've received in the past. For example, you may have been told, "Your thinking is too black and white," a description that does not exactly align with the words I chose. However, you will find this depiction is actually part of the superpower of "precise and rigid." Each superpower description explains the different ways the overused strength and its impact on others can be interpreted. Therefore, be certain to read each description to determine if there is an aspect that might belong to you.

Another reason to read each superpower is that although it may not be limiting you right now, you may find it is one you want to monitor to keep the behaviors and outcomes within acceptable tolerance limits. Every person exhibits each of the destructive powers of every overused strength at some point. These can show up even when it is not the leader's overused strength, for example, when the individual is exhausted or under extreme stress. Pay attention to your clear superpowers, but also be aware of the others so that you can course correct any negative behaviors if they pop into your repertoire.

Egotistical and Manipulative

You might be surprised that the negative descriptors of egotistical and manipulative are not among the top ten. This is because any of the superpowers can be perceived as egotistical or manipulative. These are labels we give to others when their actions seem self-serving rather than for the good of the organization. Egotistical or manipulative defines the assumed motive of the individual, not the behavior itself.

Ego itself is not bad. Every human being has an ego and a brain that is built for survival. That flight-or-fight response in each person is not worried about saving the species; it is worried about keeping the one body attached to it alive. If an individual were altruistic all the time, the person would avoid conflict and yield to others' needs. He would end up exhausted and die from hunger from meeting everyone else's desires.

Leaders also require a stronger ego than others in the organization. They must believe that they are the best choice from among their peers to step up and take charge. They have to be confident in their ability to have others willingly follow their direction.

Sometimes others who are envious of the leader's confidence unjustly give him a label of egotistical or manipulative. However, when a strength is amplified far beyond the needs of the situation, it is no longer serving the group as a whole. Instead, the behavior is serving the perceived safety and survival needs of the leader. The leader is protecting his hard-earned beliefs. There are times when superpowers can get to this level, and I've provided examples within each chapter of superpowers being interpreted as egotistical and manipulative.

Acknowledging the Gift

A superpower is a gift for yourself and your company. You don't want to eliminate the beneficial behaviors; you just want to tone it down so that it doesn't become destructive, distracting, or uncomfortable for you or for others. The Hulk's strength is still a gift—but a more appreciated gift at a less-intense level.

Think about someone who has presented you with a gift, but when you opened it, it was just too much. Perhaps he spent a lot or just overwhelmed you with too many things. Perhaps you viewed it as inappropriate for the circumstances. It's not that you don't want the person to give a gift in the future; it's just that you want him to do it differently so it doesn't result in awkwardness for either of you. Likewise, your company wants you to bring your gift; they just want you to eliminate the unintended consequences by doing it differently. Remember this as you find your superpower. Don't focus on eliminating it. Instead, embrace it so that, as you work through the book, you can increase its effectiveness by decreasing its intensity.

Ready to keep those natural defenses down and discover your wonderful strength and its potential overuse?

Download the superpower checklist and other tools at www.theinsightfulleader.com/book-bonuses to assist you in your discovery as you work through the chapters.

Take a deep breath to quiet the survival brain, and prepare to pull back the bow and lift the lid to uncover your gifts.

CHAPTER REMINDERS

- **Listen to Your Body:** Notice when your flight-or-fight response is triggered, and challenge your protective thinking.

- **Intention Doesn't Always Equal Perception:** Your desired outcome and other peoples' experiences of that outcome are two different things. Pay attention to when the two are not aligned.

- **Ask "What" Instead of "Why":** This will help reduce your self-protecting defenses when trying to find the source of your superpower.

- **Take a Deep Breath:** If you start to feel anxious, breathe deeply. This inhalation will tell your mind that you are not in a survival situation. You will be able to return to your higher-thinking functions and analyze perceptions more rationally.

- **More Than One Superpower:** Be on the lookout for multiple superpowers. Your adversity experiences usually give more than one gift.

PART 2

The Superpowers

I am thankful for my struggle because without it, I wouldn't have stumbled across my strength.

—Alexandra Elle, American author,
Words from a Wanderer

CHAPTER THREE

Results-Oriented or Impractical

Striving for excellence is stimulating and rewarding. Striving for perfection—in practically anything—is both neurotic and futile.
—Edwin C. Bliss, author of *Doing It Now* and *Getting Things Done*

Results-oriented leaders don't want to hear excuses or how busy someone is or even how hard the person is trying. They want tangible outcomes they can measure. They want this from others, but even more so, they want it from themselves. There will be no excuses for missing a deadline, not achieving a goal, or falling short of a performance target. In their minds, the minimum is meeting requirements, and the true measure of success is exceeding those expectations.

It's easy to see why an organization promotes results-oriented individuals into positions of leadership. Their bosses know they can rely on these leaders to get the job done right and on time. If there is a challengingly tight deadline, these leaders will meet it. If there is an overload of work, these leaders will volunteer to assist. In return, they receive the outstanding performance reviews and bonuses they crave as proof of their value to the organization.

Continued recognition can create an addiction to surpassing targets. Soon, instead of trying to beat the success measures of a few key priorities, they have applied their high standards to every priority set for them. In their minds, it is no longer acceptable to just meet expectations for any of their outcomes—they have to surpass all of them. These leaders are going to give 110 percent to every effort. Anything less is just not good enough. They will do whatever it takes to reach these self-imposed hurdles, including working long hours and weekends. It is not uncommon for these conquest-driven leaders to talk about a demanding schedule for both their work and personal lives. These leaders will rise early in the morning to work out, make the kids a healthy breakfast, pack a healthy lunch, or do whatever they perceive *needs* to be done to meet their own high standards. In the evenings, they have created a similar hectic routine where they squeeze in a few more hours of work before retiring for the night. On the weekends, these leaders have mentally scheduled in a block of hours for reengaging in work. Come Sunday, they either rise early or devote their evening to catching up on e-mails or advancing a project. Although results-oriented leaders may believe they are disengaging from work on the weekends, this is a fallacy. Every once in a while, in the back of their minds, when they are involved with friends or families, a little reminder pops up of how much they still have to accomplish. It's like a low-level anxiety plaguing their days of supposed rest.

This anxiety is rooted in the adversity experienced earlier in life. At some point, these leaders believed that meeting someone's real or imagined expectations was extremely critical to getting some basic need met. Perhaps being good enough was required for their survival or ability to obtain love, food, money, health, or a sense of belonging. Although this previous experience is long past, these leaders are still trying to meet the haunting expectations.

When these achievement-oriented leaders are asked if they expect the same level of results from their direct staff, they will answer, "Of course not." At some level of consciousness, they know the outcomes they have set for themselves are unrealistic. These supercharged leaders may believe they are only holding themselves to this impractical performance standard, but unfortunately, this is an illusion. Their direct reports are paying more attention to their leaders' behavior than to their words.

If the direct reports don't hear an enthusiastic "Awesome!", "Outstanding!", "You nailed it!", or "You rocked it!" from their boss, they know they didn't rise to the occasion. They know their leader would never be happy with a "Good job" or "Nicely done." They are well aware that their leader would decipher a mildly enthusiastic response as being merely adequate. Therefore, the team members interpret this feedback with the same lens—if it doesn't rise to the boss's personal standards, it isn't good enough. The entire team begins burdening themselves with their leader's unrealistic expectations.

Peers view these outcome-driven leaders as workaholics whose intense focus sets an impractical precedent that cannot be sustained. They resent these unsatisfied leaders' perceived attempts to take over joint tasks and projects in order to complete the work faster or with higher quality than necessary. Those colleagues who attempt to pace their efforts in order to avoid burnout feel judged. Peers assume these high-strung leaders believe them to be lazy, incompetent, or less committed to the outcome.

When these overzealous leaders step across clear boundaries of responsibility or decision-making authority, peers interpret their motives as starting a turf battle, and conflict ensues. Complaints by peers to the boss result in mild scolding to the usually highly praised leader to be less impatient, discuss expectations, and let others contribute. The real root of the conflict, the leader's consistently impossible high expectations, is missed because it is difficult for the boss to see how having high performance standards could be anything but positive.

Egotistical or Manipulative

A leader who feels the need to get exemplary results as fast as possible may believe that there is no time to mentor or coach someone else on meeting the essential criteria he concludes is missing. This leader assumes the quickest way to ensure a great outcome is to take ownership of the task. When this focused leader takes sole responsibility for increasing the work performance of direct reports or peers, his intrusion is met with resistance. Others assume the overinvolved leader is suggesting that only he is capable of producing at the higher level. Because the leader didn't come to them directly to clarify expectations or state concerns, the leader's behavior solidifies the perception that the leader thinks of himself as better than anyone else.

Leaders who can get their direct reports to go above and beyond are certainly assets to their organizations. One might think that with the entire team focused on doing their best, there would be much to celebrate, but this is another area where the results-oriented superpower can cause problems. For leaders who are goal oriented, each achievement brings a sense of satisfaction and success; these leaders have once again proven their value. With the previous goal met, they turn their energy and excitement to the next challenge to conquer. Unfortunately, these recent accomplishments are often celebrated internally, in the minds of these results-oriented leaders. A quick mental "Woo hoo!" and they are ready to tackle the next objective with the same gusto. There is no time like the present to get started surpassing the next hurdle. In their hurry, they forget to pause to outwardly acknowledge others who have contributed. They forget to schedule events to celebrate achievements. It's as if they assume everyone on their team is likewise internally motivated. This is a huge miss, as team members may incorrectly assume their leader doesn't believe the achievements they have worked hard to reach are worthy of honor. This can make direct reports feel like nothing they do is ever quite good enough. When this pattern becomes the norm, the team starts questioning their leader's motive. Subordinates assume their leader is withholding reward just to get them to work harder. At this point, they feel used. They start to resent the lack of external acknowledgment or even time to recover from the last burst of effort. If their leader receives recognition from next-level management for the team's accomplishments, direct reports will feel manipulated. This is when team members begin complaining about their boss getting rewarded with higher pay and bonuses for the work the team does.

The Case of Stephanie

Stephanie couldn't remember a time when she hadn't been results driven. In high school, her high standards had made her the assigned or nominated lead on many projects. She was quick to get the group organized and focused on doing what was necessary to earn an A. If someone failed to approach a portion of the assignment with the level of vigor she thought was necessary, she would put in extra effort to make up for the shortcoming.

When Stephanie started her career, her focus on exceeding expectations got her noticed, and she was quickly added to the list of high potentials. She was promoted swiftly up the management ranks. Each success brought more confidence in her abilities, and her scope was rapidly expanded. If the company wanted something done right, they knew Stephanie was the one to go to.

After a recent downsizing, Stephanie was promoted to vice president over six functional areas that used to report to two separate vice presidents. Her Monday through Friday workweek expanded to twelve-hour days with another six hours on Sunday. She was thrilled her company had entrusted her with so much responsibility, and she was very proud of her title and scope. She understood that the company needed her to get results from each of her functions. Stephanie would often reiterate with her team the statement being shared at the executive level by saying, "We need to do more with less." This put added pressure on her directors to not only strive to meet her expected 110 percent outcome on every objective, but also to come in early or stay late to do it. They apologized to Stephanie when they needed to leave on time to pick up kids or squeeze in other commitments. They worried that she would perceive their on-time exit as a lack of commitment.

Stephanie felt as if she was managing forty spinning plates. She had an image in her head of a circus performer from the 1960s who would have fifteen dishes whirling on top of long sticks. The performer would run from one end of the line of plates to the other, quickly grabbing the side of each plate and flicking his wrist to keep each twirling as he went. Then the performer would run back to the end of the line to add another spinning plate. This frantic running up and down the line of plates would continue until the performer took a bow or one of the plates stopped spinning and broke.

Stephanie was afraid one of her plates would break, and the frantic running was wearing her and her team out. Soon her team started complaining to others in the company about the number of hours and the amount of work that was expected of them. Stephanie was portrayed as a taskmaster who pushed her team too hard and had unrealistic expectations.

Stephanie's boss brought her into the office and told her the feedback circulating among the company. The boss apologized for adding to the problem by putting too much under Stephanie's scope and suggested he move some of her responsibilities to another vice president. Stephanie interpreted this to mean that her boss thought she was not performing at a high-enough level. She was extremely proud that her scope was larger than the other vice president's, so she pleaded with her boss to not adjust her workload. The senior vice president could see that Stephanie was extremely concerned about the suggestion and agreed not to make a change for three more months to see how it worked out. Stephanie swore she would get her arms around the multitude of projects and bring the workload into a manageable range. In Stephanie's mind, her plan of attack included adding more work hours to her days and weekends. She rationalized that she would put in the extra hours on Sunday, when her boyfriend was usually relaxing watching football on TV. She hated being idle and found it difficult to sit with him, anyway.

Stephanie quickly learned that this was not a sustainable solution. She was exhausted, and the added stress made her lose patience even more quickly than usual. Her boss became frustrated and suggested that she might have unrealistic expectations of how much she could handle. Stephanie was devastated at this feedback. This was proof that she still wasn't good enough.

Getting Back in Balance

If you envision spinning plates, diving catches for the ball, and juggling multiple priorities, and you know you are spending way too many hours trying to make it all happen, then you are one of the many leaders who have an overactive results-driven focus.

You may be thinking that I'm going to tell you to let go of some of your priorities and delegate them to someone else. If you can do that, great! However, most leaders haven't made it up the career ladder without learning to delegate, so that is usually not the issue. Instead, challenge your mind's desire to reach 110 percent on every deliverable. Ask yourself, "Is it absolutely true that I need to deliver every outcome I'm responsible for at 110 percent or even 100 percent?"

Think about this. At the end of the year, how many outcomes do you get to mention during your performance review? Perhaps three or maybe five?

Your company and the boss are most interested in those outcomes that directly tie to key strategies, increased revenue, reduced expenses, or reduced legal risk. The rest are important, but they don't require a stellar performance. Thinking back to your last performance review, how many of your outstanding accomplishments were highlighted in the session? Most likely, it was only a fraction. For all those other accomplishments, your efforts were appreciated but were not worthy of spending extra time revisiting what an outstanding job you did.

Likewise, when you compare your outstanding review to your peers who also received outstanding reviews, did they work as intensely as you did at every project they were responsible for? Did they drive their team as hard? Did they spend the same amount of hours focused on work?

You are now recognizing that you could have reached the same end-of-year outcome by focusing on exceeding expectations on the few key outcomes that were the company's highest priority and setting a goal of meeting expectations for other important results. There were probably a few expectations that you could have even negotiated to do at lower outcome levels than you initially set for yourself.

As you set your objectives and goals for the year, keep in mind that not everything has to be done to the highest of standards. Look back through your list of objectives and find a few where ensuring they are completed would suffice. Avoid imposing a quality level that is going to create more work than the effort is worth. Also, consider a reasonable cadence of work. For a few of the objectives, perhaps the first-year goal is getting a sturdy foundation built, and then the following year you can bring the project to award-winning levels.

Here is a really radical idea to curb your need to surpass expectations: let something be adequate. Your mind chatter is probably going nuts at the notion of trying this. You may even feel that this would be allowing yourself to fail, but let me explain. Others will not interpret what you currently see as a failure so harshly. Getting a C is not failure; it's trending with the norm. Likewise, earning a mark of "meeting expectations" is not equivalent to mediocrity. Take one of your objectives that is not critical to the organization's future and complete it at an average level. Make certain the stated expectations are met, but no extra jumping through hoops. See what happens in terms of feedback. You're going to notice that it doesn't make your boss or your leaders think less of you. At the year's end, you will see it does not enter into the performance review. This is because your company would rather have you ensure the few essential projects are done extremely well than dilute your energy on everything within your scope.

You may be saying that this is all fine and good, but your boss is also a results-driven leader and expects nothing short of amazing from you and your team. If that's the case, assess if you and your team can realistically sustain all the effort and hours for another year without burning out. It's easy for the great performers to be burdened with more work and responsibilities. Determine if you are misinterpreting this as recognizing your gifts rather than your boss unintentionally placing impractical expectations on you while other leaders get a workload that is more manageable. Inadvertently, your boss is punishing great work. If you are certain that you are not attempting to meet everything at an outstanding level and the workload is truly unrealistic, speak up. Let your boss know you appreciate the faith shown in you. Then explain that by adding more projects, you will need to either drop something off this year's priorities or renegotiate the expected quality level of one or more of your objectives. If that is not possible, then you will need more resources or time. Be clear that you and your team cannot sustain the number of hours and intensity of the workload without burning out. Do not see it as your boss reinforcing how great you are. Being given more challenging assignments may be desirable, but expanding your workload for exceeding past expectations is not an appropriate reward.

Now flip this same conversation and envision your team coming to you concerned about their workload. Do you have any high-results individuals on your team who you are inadvertently punishing with more projects and higher expectations that will require excessive hours? Make certain you are not guilty of placing the same burden on your high performers.

At some point, your past adversity resulted in attempting to meet someone else's perceived or real expectations. This has morphed into trying to meet your own exaggerated expectations. Recognize that the person your subconscious is striving to impress is not at work or at home; it is just you.

Are you being unkind to yourself?

Would you want to work for you?

Keep bringing your A+ approach to the outcomes that most benefit the organization and your family. Let the other outcomes suffice with a B or C. Those put on the succession plan are not always the honor students or class valedictorians. They are the leaders who get results by being more balanced in their approach. They are the leaders who demonstrate that they can maintain a high level of output year after year without exhausting their teams.

GETTING BACK IN BALANCE REMINDERS

- **Determine the Critical Few:** Review your priorities and find the few that would benefit the company most. Put your extra effort into these.
- **Reprogram Your Thinking:** Stop equating meeting expectations or doing an adequate job with being mediocre or a failure.
- **Speak Up:** If you have a results-oriented boss who is reinforcing your unrealistic expectations, speak up, and renegotiate priorities, quality, time, or resources.
- **Stop Punishing High Performers:** Check to ensure you are not inadvertently punishing your great performers with added work and stress.

CHAPTER FOUR

Problem Finder or Pessimist

We can complain because rose bushes have thorns, or rejoice
because thorn bushes have roses.
—Jean-Baptiste Alphonse Karr, French journalist, critic,
and novelist, *A Tour Round My Garden*

The problem finder who can quickly call out errors and potential problems and identify all the possible negative outcomes of a course of action is a huge asset to any company. Having someone who can forewarn the team that the recommended path is wrought with barriers or potential pitfalls enables the team to avoid wasting time, money, and resources on the wrong solutions. The critical evaluator's mind, equipped with a multitude of decision trees, figures out possible alternatives and outcomes, calculates the risk factors and probabilities, and proudly shares all the possible negative scenarios for consideration.

It is not surprising that when critical evaluators join a group or organization, they often receive praise for their ability. They are asked to lead numerous projects and task forces. Others begin to rely on their ability to point out the likely obstacles. This gift gets stronger with consecutive reinforcement until these leaders start to see their role as the designated problem finder.

At this point, these critical evaluators can't seem to keep their brains from quickly pointing out holes, missing information, problems, and discrepancies. Their language becomes increasingly absolute as their certainty in their gift grows. When they first brought their skills to the team, the problem finders' wording was investigative, and their tone was gentle, but now they speak of impending doom in an almost accusatory tone.

"We might have a potential problem with the alignment of these two factors" becomes "There is no way we will be successful because these two factors are not aligned."

The former rendition invited others to find possible solutions to reach successful completion. The latter version implies that there is an impassable roadblock.

With this change, others no longer see these leaders as constructively confronting the possible issues; they see these critical evaluators as crying warnings that may or may not be true. The foreboding scenarios are viewed as throwing roadblocks in the way and attempting to stall progress rather than partnering to reach a successful outcome.

Somewhere along the way, these leaders have moved from assessing the potential and probability of failure to believing they are responsible for keeping the organization risk-free. Their heightened focus on the possible negative consequences overshadows any positive outcome. The risky choice that also has a possibility of reaping great rewards is no longer a factor in the equation. Opportunities are missed. They are too focused on the doom-and-gloom scenarios.

Soon, these gifted problem solvers stop receiving invitations to lead or participate in new projects. Organizers, in an effort to preserve the excitement and optimistic energy on their teams, determine it is better not to invite naysaying leaders to the first phase of meetings. There is concern that these pessimistic leaders will derail the projects in a downward discussion of what won't work. Their invitations are delayed till the team has moved into discussing possible approaches to execution. The project team is relieved, but these gifted problem solvers are left confused as to why they were not brought in to projects earlier.

Problem-solving leaders may also experience this same exclusion when executives quickly convene a group of leaders to assess, analyze, and solve a major company problem. The executives may say they need to select leaders who have a positive can-do attitude to justify the exclusion of the leader. However, their real concern is that the pessimistic leader, in an effort to convince others that the options are just too perilous, misses assessing the risk of maintaining the status quo. This omission can be a quicker path to failure if existing problems require immediate resolution. These executives can't afford to wait for the perfect, risk-free solution.

When leading their teams, supercharged problem solvers often scrutinize the work of their direct reports. Their motive may be developing their team, but this backfires when their members feel that every aspect of their work is criticized in excruciating detail. Not only the concepts in the proposal but also the wording choices and sequencing are critiqued.

These leaders tell their direct reports that their intense examination is to ensure nothing important is missed. Ironically, these leaders have over-looked something very important—telling the team members what they did well. This imbalance of feedback leads to team members feeling as if their work is never good enough. Team members begin to believe their leader finds them incapable. After a while, frustrated team members join forces to condemn their leader's analysis of their work. Team members counterattack by nitpicking their leader's work and gleefully pointing out the faults. When the team's frustration mounts, members start complaining about their leader's perceived lack of trust outside of the department.

These leaders' constant identification of potential problems can also erode their boss's patience. These leaders may learn that their gift has gone too far when they hear statements from their superiors such as, "I'm assigning you and your team this project. I don't want to hear about why it can't be done. I want you to uncover the issues and solve them." These problem solvers don't believe they are as fatalistic as their bosses imply; therefore, they interpret their bosses' tone as undeserved.

As these shifts begin to happen, these leaders start to notice people addressing them in a defensive tone. This resistance creates confusion, because, in these critical evaluators' minds, they are only trying to help others and the company put their best thoughts and solutions forward. The negative feedback and advice provided are directed at the work, not at individuals. They wonder how anyone could perceive their responses as an insult. However, a critical evaluator's barrage of objections, without the balance of recognizing what is good, feels like a personal attack on character, intelligence, and assumed motive to those who have become defensive. Ironically, in a similar twist, these critical evaluators interpret others' defensive responses as a criticism of their analysis, intellect, and motive.

Egotistical or Manipulative

Critical evaluators can be seen as egotistical when their motives are interpreted as proving their intellectual superiority. Others assume the leader believes only she can identify and solve the group's problems when the overamplified leader quickly finds fault with whatever is proposed. This is not often the case but instead a perception created by overuse.

This superpower can also be seen as manipulative if the leader asks others for their recommendations, dismisses each option, and then proposes a different solution. This behavior may give others the impression that the leader wanted to implement her solution from the beginning and had no real intention of taking anyone else's ideas into consideration. Team members can feel as if their efforts were a waste of time. The original intention of the leader may have been to be consultative in her approach; however, by discrediting each suggestion in its entirety rather than acknowledging what was positive and possible with each suggestion, the leader has unintentionally created this impression of manipulating the team into buying into the leader's idea. The leader can avoid this misperception if she stops to give credit to others for strong rationale and acknowledges any ideas incorporated into the final recommendation.

The Case of David

David was a brilliant engineer. He had this uncanny ability to mentally take anything apart and put it back together in endless configurations, each time determining the pros and cons of every alternative. His intellectual and technical abilities got him noticed early in his career, and he was promoted into management quickly. He continued to see problems and solutions others had not considered, and in a few years, he was promoted to director and eventually to vice president. The company needed his brilliance and ability to call out potential problems.

It was shortly after being promoted to vice president that David's leadership team started complaining to the executives. His ability to rattle off potential roadblocks and problems became amplified to decibel levels that were abrasive to his team and others. The team had already experienced quite a bit of turnover, so the rest of David's directors didn't find it too risky to let David's boss, the senior vice president, know that David was not only frustrating to work for but also perceived as arrogant. When they brought recommendations to him, they felt his endless listing of potential issues assumed they had not considered these possible impacts. They interpreted his challenges of their proposals as publicly belittling their capabilities. His team and others assumed that David thought he was smarter than everyone else, that only he could analyze and solve complex problems. They also didn't feel David had any vested interest in developing their capabilities.

David's boss started noticing that, in meetings, the rest of the vice presidents expected David to have something negative to say anytime a proposal was vetted. The presenter would state the issue, provide a recommendation, and open the discussion to questions and opinions. All eyes would turn to David in anticipation of him challenging some aspect of the presentation. David's peers knew that if they waited, David would bring up their own concerns, taking away the burden of them being seen as unsupportive of the proposal. This just added to a wider company perspective of David as a negative person.

None of these outcomes were David's intention, but his team was grasping for a reason why David was so hypercritical of their proposals and solutions. They had no idea of David's real reasons for having such a heightened survival mode of finding the problems "before it was too late." David's boss told him he needed to eliminate his reputation of being "overly negative and arrogant."

David was shocked by this feedback and felt it was unfair, since he saw himself as focused on solving problems. He could not think of a time when he had sought recognition for his accomplishments.

Over the next few months, David attempted to contain his overprotective desire to identify weaknesses. He kept telling himself to find opportunities to recognize what was positive, but it felt contrived. He felt as if he was attempting to say something affirming, but he knew he was just biding time till he could once again critique.

David also noticed that at home he was equally judgmental about his spouse and children. There was so much he loved about his family, so he was surprised at how often he critiqued them rather than expressed what he appreciated. He felt like his brain was playing a constant game of What's Wrong with This Picture. He wanted to stop hunting for the negatives and see the whole picture.

Getting Back in Balance

If you could identify with any of the previous descriptors of the pessimist or even David's story, you are not alone. Finding problems is a commonly overused strength of many leaders. The adversity that taught you to analyze situations quickly to foresee the next previously hidden trap served you well. This ability also serves your team and company—when kept within tolerable limits.

To get your gift back in balance, recognize that others already acknowledge you as a great problem finder. You no longer have to prove this value to the organization. Now you must prove that you are looking at problems from the view of an optimist rather than a pessimist.

Shift your image of your role. Rather than seeing yourself as the great analyzer who can ferret out problems, see yourself as the great facilitator for solving dilemmas. Focus more on working with others to find solutions rather than problem hunting on your own.

Set a rule for yourself that you cannot raise a problematic issue until you find something about the proposal to like. Nothing will cure your perceived imbalance faster than forcing yourself to comment on what is right before harping on what is wrong. This technique also rewires your problem-finder brain to become the creative problem solver. Identifying the opportunities requires your mind to shift from answering the question "What is wrong with this proposal?" to "What do I like about this proposal, and how do we keep these advantages while avoiding the dangers?" This modification takes you from pessimist to data-driven optimist.

Another advantage of focusing on what is right is that it allows you to expound on someone else's good thoughts and recommendations. It will make the solution a collaborative effort and increase the speed of acceptance.

To remember to use this technique, write the reminder "First find what is right" in a place where you can see it. Write it in a notebook you use for meetings, post it to your computer, place it by your phone, or put it on your bathroom mirror. Think of all the places you could use this reminder: in project meetings, staff meetings, phone conversations, composing e-mails, or in one-on-one meetings with the boss. Go beyond work, and think about where else you could use this reminder. Perhaps it would be helpful when critiquing your kid's homework or your spouse's ideas for a home renovation project. An out-of-balance critical evaluator at work is often a critical evaluator at home.

Making this transition to focusing on the positive and going from problem finder to problem solver will also require you to identify your source of adversity and challenge your deeply held beliefs. Your brain has equated foreseeing possible complications with avoidance of pain and successful survival. Your past life and career successes have honed these skills and reinforced the belief that you are the only person you can rely on to complete this critical task.

Challenge these beliefs.

What beliefs do you hold that reinforce your assumption that you must be the one to identify problems? Which of these thoughts are valid and which may be faulty assumptions?

For example, you may believe the following:

- I'm very skilled at critical analysis.
- If I don't speak up about the issue, no one else will.
- The company has put me in a role that requires I play the part of critical evaluator.

The first statement is probably very true. You are skilled at it. After all, you've probably taken on this role for yourself and others for a very long time.

The second statement is an assumption. You won't know if it is true that no one else will speak up unless you stop playing the role of critical evaluator and give others an opportunity to raise their concerns. You may have unconsciously trained people to let you speak up about these issues. If you keep doing it, people will continue to rely on you to continue this behavior. If they see the boss's eyes roll when you unconsciously go into a pessimistic rant, they may equate bringing up potentially bad news as being negative and therefore decide, either consciously or unconsciously, to allow you to continue to carry this burden. You may argue that you have tried keeping quiet and letting others raise the dire issues, but if you've assumed this role for quite some time, one or two efforts at silence are not going to send a strong-enough message that you expect others to take over your role. You are going to need to be more explicit in your changed expectations.

The third statement about your role requiring this behavior is false. It is not your role. Think about all the leaders you know who don't assume this duty to the extent you do. How many leaders see their role as finding viable solutions, not finding potential problems? The leader's role is to describe the objective and rally the team to find the best pathways to reach the end point. Your role does require expertise, critical thinking, and weighing pros and cons, but it does *not* require the leader to be the person who thinks of everything. Let others on your team gain the positive skills of critical evaluation.

Your gift can be a wonderful opportunity to coach others in these critical-thinking skills. Rather than telling them the potential problems with their proposal, ask them questions to let them discover them on their own. When your mind's squirrel starts its warning chirps of "That will never work! It will be disastrous," quiet it with a deep breath. Instead of spouting off all proof of impending doom, flip your role to coach. Instead of telling, ask questions—after acknowledging the positive.

For example, "Your recommendation to change our process to increase our speed of output has some great ideas, specifically . . . " Add particulars so the person knows you are not just giving them a pat on the head.

As your brain focuses on the negatives and rattles off objections with the proposal, change them to questions: "How would you propose we solve this issue?" "How do you think your change would affect the customer?" "I'm concerned about this variable. What do you think we could do to address this issue?"

One of two things will happen. Either the individual will come to the same conclusion that the proposal is not yet a viable solution or she will surprise you with a great solution that you had not considered. Both are winning outcomes. Asking questions also sends a message that you believe the individual is worth coaching and developing. Showing this concern for the team member will help you regain her trust and respect.

None of this advice is asking you to remain quiet when a flaw exists and no one else sees it. Your gift is still of great value. When you do choose to engage it, ensure it adds value and in a way that reinforces the positive attributes of the recommendation.

This quote by author C. Joybell C. provides a great reminder: "Choose your battles wisely. After all, life isn't measured by how many times you stood up to fight. It's not winning battles that makes you happy, but it's how many times you turned away and chose to look into a better direction. Life is too short to spend it on warring. Fight only the most, most, most important ones, let the rest go."

GETTING BACK IN BALANCE REMINDERS

- **Let Others Rise to the Challenge:** Recognize that the role of problem finder is not yours alone. Give others an opportunity to raise potential issues and problems.

- **Notice What Is Right:** Don't criticize until you can acknowledge or appreciate at least one thing about someone else's suggestion or recommended solution.

- **Find Opportunities:** Find ways to turn problems into opportunities. If you can solve a major challenge, you may have just discovered the next big thing.

- **Expand on Others' Ideas:** Rather than believing you need to have the answer, stay open to others' inputs and suggestions. Acknowledge good ideas and build upon these thoughts to overcome any foreseeable issues.

- **Share Your Skills:** Coach others in your problem-finding skills so they can critique their recommendations before sharing them.

CHAPTER FIVE

Intellectually Curious or Know-It-All

The mind is not a vessel to be filled, but a fire to be kindled.
—Plutarch, ancient Greek historian

Individuals who love to learn become lifelong students. They are eager to discover new ideas and seek a variety of sources to continue their accumulation of knowledge. This exploration of new facts, theories, and connections is either focused on specific areas of interest or across a breadth of topics. These intellectually curious leaders become excited when they gain insight into something new or learn a twist to previous knowledge. They are the expert-on-call when others need to check a fact or complete missing information. They research to find answers to perplexing problems. They are also a huge advantage to the company when they provide the latest information on trends affecting the business or supply previously unknown data that can change the course of a project's direction.

When working in peer groups, these intellectually curious leaders assume others will be equally interested and inspired in their newly discovered database; therefore, they generously share their new proficiency. When the amount of information is in line with the needs of the group, all parties are engaged and immersed in a sense of wonder as members exclaim, "I didn't know that!" The group finds the information applicable to the topic being discussed and helpful to the group's progress. Leaders with this superpower interpret this reaction as proof that they should share even more information. Reinforced, these leaders start to provide other tangential wisdom. They continue to interject facts into conversations and interrupt to contribute their wealth of knowledge. Their sentence starters become predictable—"Did you know . . . ?", "I just read that . . . ", and "A recent article on . . ." Their enthusiasm for their learning and their desire to spread this knowledge is admirable, but it becomes too much.

Barely audible sighs of frustration and upward eye glances between listeners communicate an unspoken "Here we go again," signaling to each other they have had enough. Listeners finally revert to interrupting these avid learners midsentence to try to get the conversation back on topic. At this saturation point, assumptions are made about these leaders' motives. Many believe they are trying to prove their intellectual superiority. In contrast, these supercharged leaders interpret the group's dismissal of the information as proof that their peers do not comprehend the importance or wisdom of what is being said. These leaders respond with unconscious, nonverbal agitation. Their frustrated replies fuel peers' assumptions that these leaders believe they are smarter.

When these intellectually curious leaders use their superpower with their direct reports, their motives are interpreted slightly differently. In an effort to grow the team, these leaders are compelled to provide not only the highlights of their fascinating discoveries but also the details and nuances. What is expected to be a quick explanation of a current challenge becomes a soliloquy rambling on while direct reports squirm uncomfortably in their chairs. A scheduled five-minute kickoff to a team problem-solving meeting results in "Can you believe this?" glances when the team is held captive for a fifteen-minute lecture. This overenthusiastic sharing earns these leaders labels of "little professor" or "sage on the stage." Direct reports start to dread these interactions they perceive as 20 percent value and 80 percent waste of time.

Providing feedback to these supercharged leaders can be difficult because these leaders just can't compute how knowledge could be anything but beneficial. Frustrated direct reports eventually take their complaints to their leader's boss. When a boss informs the leader of the perceptions, she deflects the feedback, stating it was done to provide guidance and coaching. The leader argues that her role is to expand the team's knowledge and skills. Both boss and leader leave the meeting exasperated.

The best chance for feedback to make its way through these leaders' defenses is having it come from a respected colleague, coach, or superior not directly aligned to the leader—someone the leader believes has unbiased reasons for giving corrective evaluation. Even with this respected relationship, though, the leader is still shocked to learn she is sharing more information than the situation warrants.

Egotistical or Manipulative

These intellectually curious leaders can be seen as egotistical after continuing to ramble on when others believe they have communicated to the individual that the conversation has persisted for too long. As agitation mounts, the listeners become more convinced in their theory that the leader is trying to showcase knowledge to prove highly advanced thinking. Most of the time this is not the case. Rolling of eyes; sighing heavily; clearing throats; shifting in seats; looking at watches, cellphones, or laptops; and attempting to interrupt are cues that can be missed by the content-focused leader. The perceived know-it-all is often not sensitive to these social signs of impatience and disapproval.

If asked if anyone communicated impatience with the input, these leaders may mention one or two individuals who might not have understood the importance of what was being said but often do not see the collective anguish of the rest of the listeners. These leaders will argue that if some were frustrated, those individuals should have spoken up about it. However, someone speaking up to tell these lovers of learning that their content is not applicable to the immediate needs of the discussion may not solve the problem. These leaders may not extrapolate that the feedback applies to conversations beyond the current one. This critical comment may get them to stop immediately sharing, but unless someone follows up to explain that this is a pattern that needs to be modified, these leaders will likely be overly verbose again. Repetition of the behavior will just fuel assumptions that these leaders are incapable of changing because of their assumed superiority.

When these leaders are overseeing their direct reports or are put in charge of projects, perceptions can escalate to manipulation. Their oversharing can be misinterpreted as trying to take over the project or trying to claim all the credit for the group's outcomes. These leaders may have intended to assign the project to the team members and let them complete it; however, as these leaders keep interjecting with "interesting" facts and backstory, it appears they are trying to prove the project cannot be done without their guidance. If a team is reporting their recommendations to key decision makers and their leader interjects with details and tidbits, it can be perceived as their leader not allowing the team to have their moment of glory and as trying to assume credit. If these information-driven leaders were told about these impressions that they are manipulative, they would be shocked that anyone would deduce this from their well-meaning attempts to share their knowledge for the greater good.

These intellectually curious leaders can be perceived as both egotistical and manipulative when they seemingly play games of one-upmanship. A colleague may challenge their logic, a boss may disagree with their recommendation, or a peer may tease them about a weakness. This questioning of abilities can unconsciously trigger unpleasant memories of being challenged or bullied. In response to these perceived threats, they whip out their biggest weapon—their intellect. The unsuspecting person has suddenly found himself in a dual of wits where the winner is the last one standing. These intellects' goal is to have their statements in any conversation be so compelling that they make the other person yield to their logic. These know-it-alls fire information forth, asserting that these bullets of facts are valid conclusions (whether they are or not). This barrage continues until the other person yields from exhaustion, saying, "I'm not going to argue with you anymore." In these know-it-alls' rationalization, the opponent's inability to respond with additional proof is confirmation of their exceptional brilliance. With this intense superpower, they fail to consider that the other individual may not be responding because that person recognizes the fruitlessness of the conversation or has tired of the game.

After the encounter, these know-it-alls may tell others of their conquests. They are confident the other person could not hold their own in the debate and allude to the fact that their opponent wasn't as smart as they are. Ironically, these supercharged know-it-alls have failed to understand how brilliant the other person was to discontinue the no-win diatribe. They also fail to realize the reputation they are creating for themselves as intellectual bullies.

The Case of Mark

Mark was interested in learning everything he could about his area of expertise, cybersecurity. He read every evening, attended conferences, and subscribed to the latest research. In addition to his own area of study, he was also interested in the broader fields of technology and science. Some would describe him as a walking Wikipedia, but he would have argued that his data was more current and more accurate. To him, this was just a statement of fact.

When Mark wasn't spending his spare time reading, he was hanging out with like-minded friends who loved a great discussion and an even greater debate. One bit of knowledge would spark another, one idea would counter another, and one shared experience would spur the sharing of another. These discussions and debates could go on for hours. To an outsider, it might appear that each of the friends didn't really listen to the others. One person would hardly be done sharing a view when another would interject with some tangential idea. This volley back and forth was perfectly acceptable to those involved.

When Mark tried these same behaviors at work with his peers, they became agitated with his interruptions and told him he wasn't listening. They were obviously frustrated with him, but he assumed they were really frustrated because they didn't understand the depth of knowledge he was attempting to share. He felt restricted to being the cybersecurity geek when he possessed a breadth and depth of knowledge about many subjects.

His direct reports were likewise frustrated by Mark's perceived know-it-all behavior. They complained to Mark's boss, who decided to attend one of Mark's staff meetings to observe his behaviors.

Mark entered the glass conference room at the start of the hour to kick off a new project with his team. Several times during his explanation of the project expectations, he veered into monologues sharing his experiences on previous projects and what those had taught him. When he asked the team questions about their knowledge on different aspects of the project, he would get the input of one or two people and then quickly share his seemingly more extensive knowledge. There were perhaps others on the team who could have added to the discussion, but they were not given the opportunity. It was obvious from Mark's proud stance that he believed he was at his best when he was sharing information.

After the meeting, Mark's boss told him he overcoached his employees. Mark was surprised; after all, he believed this was one of his best traits as a leader. She told Mark that as a director, his team was surprisingly inexperienced. He said he preferred this so he could take them under his wing. He believed that one of his greatest assets was coaching and increasing the knowledge of his direct reports. When asked about his high turnover of seasoned team members, Mark replied that these individuals had learned what they needed from him and left his department to help other areas of the company with the knowledge they had gained. Mark's boss shared that, in actuality, several of those who transferred to other areas complained to her of feeling disrespected and belittled. She said that Mark just didn't know when to stop coaching and when to let people grow on their own. She added that she could no longer accept the high turnover of experienced personnel from his area. The loss of senior employees meant that his junior employees had to rely on him to fix the more complex problems. Since Mark was already busy, this often resulted in a delay in getting things corrected quickly. If he had had more experienced employees on his team, he could have had these individuals serve as mentors to junior team members and free Mark's time for more executive-level responsibilities. She also let him know that he needed to rebuild relationships with his peers. Mark argued that these were just misunderstandings, but his boss insisted he change his ways.

Mark was unsure of what he needed to do to change his behavior and still be the effective leader he thought he was. What was the value of knowledge if not to share it?

Getting Back in Balance

If being intellectually curious is your superpower, you already have a strong value for and command of educational intelligence. However, educational intelligence is just one of three intelligences important to leadership success. The other two are social and emotional intelligence.

You may find yourself weak on social intelligence, especially if as a child you socialized with other highly educationally intelligent children or your interactions were limited to adults who reinforced your love of knowledge. Social intelligence includes the knowledge of social roles, rules, and norms. It also comprises effective listening skills. When social intelligence is weak, the leader does not pick up on the nonverbal behaviors that communicate impatience with prolonged discourse. She also does not notice the verbal cues indicating that the conversation has moved on to another topic or line of discovery. The educationally intelligent leader is so enthralled with the current topic and excited to share her wealth of knowledge on the subject that she continues contributing to the discussion past the point of interest. She becomes overly fixated on recalling the facts and cool information connected to that topic and misses the blaring social cues. When the leader's social groups outside of work are similarly high in intellectual curiosity, the leader is isolated from the candid feedback required to hone this social intelligence.

When my son was a preteen, he was high in educational and emotional intelligence but lacked social awareness. One day he came home from school very frustrated. Apparently the class was discussing bats, a topic he was very interested in. He knew exciting things about them from a trip we had taken to Carlsbad Caverns, and he wanted to learn more. Though he asked lots of questions, the rest of the class was not engaged. After answering several of his queries, the teacher changed the subject. My son felt that his informational needs were ignored. I explained to him why the teacher did the right thing. I clarified that different people have different tolerances for depth and breadth of information as well as different interests. His teacher had noticed that the majority of the students were no longer interested and so moved on to meet their needs.

A couple of weeks later, he attended a party with me. We were talking to some parents and older kids and another topic of great interest to him came up—cloning sheep. Again, he wanted to talk longer on the subject than the rest of the group. As the group changed subjects, he tried to rekindle the previous conversation but was ignored. He took the cue from me that it was time to move on to the new topic. Afterward, he asked me why the group didn't want to keep talking about the initial subject. I agreed the conversation was interesting but told him that he needed to pay attention to the other group members to notice when they had reached their information saturation point and showed signs of boredom. We replayed the group members' nonverbal cues so he could recognize them during future encounters. Social intelligence was not something he was going to learn from his close friends, who were also very cerebral. Over time, he used his strength in emotional intelligence to pay attention and empathize with others' informational needs. Unfortunately, for many educational intellectuals weak at social intelligence, these rules of engagement are learned the hard way—as an adult bombarded with stinging feedback.

If you believe you missed out on gaining social intelligence, use your strength of research to study typical nonverbal cues and their meanings. Instead of focusing on contributing in your next meetings, take the role of a behavioral scientist observing the social interactions of a lost tribe. Assume you are not familiar with the players or the topic. Avoid any interpretation or judgment of the species. Instead, just note what the members are doing and how it elicits responses from other members of the tribe. Coming from an angle of curiosity will keep you from justifying your own behavior and open you up to seeing interactions with new knowledge and less judgment.

Emotional intelligence, on the other hand, or EQ, is the ability to understand, evaluate, and regulate both your and others' motives and emotions. It includes self-awareness and self-management. This allows you to be aware of your own feelings, such as your anger at someone judging you. EQ also enables you to regulate your response so that you stop yourself from responding defensively. Two other key components are empathy to recognize how others feel and the ability to respond with sensitivity to build relationships.

When educationally intelligent leaders lack emotional intelligence, they are unaware of how their behavior could create perceptions of superiority, distrust, or disrespect. When provided with this feedback, they cling to their own view of their intention and become defensive. This combination of lack of empathy and self-management only fuels the perception that the leaders believe they are above reproach. Often, an over-reliance on educational intelligence is quite the opposite. It's not that the leaders believe they are special or flawless but, instead, are using their knowledge to overcome known weaknesses. The leaders assume that relying on this strength will hide these defects and keep them from being singled out. This tactic backfires, since, ironically, trying to prove you are flawless results in being perceived as egotistical. Showing flaws enables others to empathize with you, since every person has them.

If you lack emotional intelligence, pay particular attention to your source of adversity in Part II of the book. Analyze your past experiences to identify ones that created a fear of rejection. This will enable you to understand how your defensiveness is on heightened alert so you can reduce your desire to protect yourself when others give you feedback. For many intellectually curious leaders, this adversity and self-defense mechanism is tied to bullying. Tell yourself that the person giving you either nonverbal or verbal feedback is not attempting to bully you. He is just expressing that right at this minute (but not always) your love of knowledge is a bit too much. Empathize with the frustration by thinking of a time when the strength of someone you know was used in excess. This will allow you to see this feedback as trying to help you become more successful versus attempting to belittle you. We all let our passion take over at times, and this makes us perfectly imperfect. Own your gifts and your imperfections to connect with others.

Now that you are more aware of the consequences of contributing too much, make a conscious effort to say only a portion of what you are thinking. Stop short of what you think others need to know, and wait for them to ask for more. Allow them to become curious. When you are invited to share more, ration it out. Watch for the nonverbal cues of interest, and take heed of the nonverbal cues of saturation. Talking less will allow you to see more. Soon, you will be able to gauge the amount of content relevant to topics and audiences.

Finally, challenge your thinking. From the time you started school, you were told knowledge would get you far, and knowledge is power. There is truth to these clichés, but sometimes not knowing is equally valuable. The amazed observer of the wondrous, iridescent, hovering hummingbird is not always better off knowing that its wings beat ten to eighty beats per second or why its throat of peacock blues and greens sparkle in the sunlight. Without this knowledge, the observer's imagination is sparked with possibilities. The observer is open to exploring, not grounded in what is. There are many times when knowledge is helpful and other times when it is a hindrance to imagination, creativity, relationships, and leadership. Use your keen ability to weigh information to determine when the time is right to share and when it is best to remain silent.

GETTING BACK IN BALANCE REMINDERS

- **Share Less:** Assume your audience wants only a quick highlight of your information. Wait for them to indicate they want more before expounding on the subject.

- **Expand Your Social Intelligence:** Study and observe nonverbal cures. Watch with curiosity the interactions of others to learn the appropriate amount of information for particular situations.

- **Expand Your Emotional Intelligence:** Take the perspective of others you interact with on a frequent basis. Assume you had their job, stressors, experiences, and values. Think about how this vantage point might affect what you need to know and your sense of urgency about the task.

- **Be Alert to Your Defensive Behavior:** When you begin to notice that you are feeling belittled or attacked, stop and ask yourself if you can be 100 percent confident that this is the other person's intention. Identify what is triggering your defensiveness.

- **Increase Your Curiosity:** Instead of focusing on facts, look at possibilities. Instead of studying what is true today, explore what could be. The facts and truths of the past are often found to be merely frameworks for future innovation.

CHAPTER SIX

Empathic or Needy

The greater your capacity to love, the greater your capacity to feel the pain.

—Jennifer Aniston, American actress

Some individuals are very emotionally sensitive. They can easily pick up on shifts in other people's feelings. Their ability to take alternative perspectives, empathize easily with others, and anticipate how they will react is a gift to the organization. They provide a much-needed balance to the analytic minds. When the company proposes a change, these leaders can predict the emotional responses and help forge a plan to reduce resistance. Without their input, the analytic minds would forge ahead and then be caught by surprise when others did not readily accept the new direction.

Sensitive leaders are also wonderful at ensuring everyone's voice is heard. If a project is going to affect other key stakeholders, they will thoughtfully bring them into the preliminary discussions. This can help the company avoid problems created by not getting unfiltered feedback early enough in the process.

These stronghearted individuals are willing to help others in need and are often described as having a lot of compassion. They can put themselves in the other person's shoes and deeply feel what it must be like to experience whatever challenges the person is facing. Instinctively knowing exactly what the person needs to hear, they forge a quick bond that enables others to disclose and feel validated. Outside of work, these strong feelers are the friends who lend a sympathetic ear and offer kindness to comfort those in pain.

When this empathic strength becomes too strong, however, the individual can argue too emotionally for the benefit of others. This can lead to perceptions of being too soft, not keeping the company's interests in mind, and being too much of an advocate for individuals. Leaders are called upon to make tough decisions that affect people's lives. It's great to anticipate and minimize reactions, but if individuals' needs weigh too heavily, they could hurt the business. If the business suffers, it could affect the livelihood of every employee. Thus, the immediate need of a few may have to be forfeited for the good of all.

When leading their direct reports, these bighearted leaders can be perceived as coddling some team members. Direct reports who tell stories of woe as reasons for not meeting deadlines or expectations strike a chord with the leader, who can easily find his own similar experience to relate. This shared empathy can result in the leader not holding individuals firmly accountable for their outcomes. The softhearted leader delays documenting the person and gives the individual additional opportunities to improve. Coworkers who are picking up the slack of the poor performer see this as unfair and get irritated with the leader. Team members tell each other that anyone who can fabricate a really good sob story doesn't have to work hard. They assume the leader lacks the backbone to act, and the leader gets labeled as weak.

Even more destructive, however, is when intensely emotionally sensitive individuals apply their empathy to their own experiences. The self-focused individual desperately cries out his perceived persecution to direct reports, peers, the boss, or anyone willing to listen.

"It's not fair. You won't believe what happened to me."

"I can't believe that someone would treat me this way."

"I'm working extremely long hours and absolutely sacrificing myself while others are coasting."

"I never get recognized."

At first, others might unwittingly participate in these empaths' negative banter. A nod in agreement, or a response of "I know how you feel," fuels these leaders' beliefs that they are seeing the world through crystal-clear lenses. Those who engage unwittingly reinforce these leaders' superpower and the catastrophic view of the situation these leaders are describing.

Having achieved validation, these intensely feeling leaders start seeking out these same individuals to validate their interpretations on other situations. When the next experience happens to them, they pop into the listener's workspace with, "Do you have a minute?" But these sharing experiences aren't short conversations. The empathic leader could go on rambling for hours if the listener doesn't cut him off with an "I have to go" statement.

Leaders with the superpower of deep empathy aren't trying to be nuisances. It's just that they feel everything at a higher intensity. That intensity is absolutely draining to others who unwittingly engage in sympathizing with them. This self-focus unintentionally creates the perception of being needy, being helpless, or assuming the role of a victim. Others describe the empathic leader's soliloquies as sucking the life energy from them. Soon those who did engage with these leaders find ways to avoid them. The leader picks up on the avoidance and fuels his feeling of victimization by believing that others are ganging up on him.

Caring leaders are great contributors to the organization, but they will get stuck at their current level once it is well known that their approach is undermining their ability to be seen as constructive problem solvers. When their names are raised in promotional discussions, eyes will roll as colleagues relive being trapped in "whiny conversations" with them. Stories of poor performers not dealt with swiftly will enter the conversation. Once the past discussions are shared, these individuals won't stand a chance, regardless of their outstanding results on projects. They get labeled as oversensitive, requiring too much attention and recognition, or not having enough fortitude for leadership.

Egotistical or Manipulative

When the empathic leader continues to complain to others about his plight, he appears needy. Having been supportive for a period of time, the listener's patience wears thin. Those who have been sucked in too many times begin to realize that the behavior is exaggerated. The listener also notices the disruption is not mutually beneficial and therefore is purely self-serving on the part of the leader. This results in the empathic leader being labeled as overly self-focused and egotistical and can easily turn to perceptions of manipulation if the other person has agreed to take some action in an effort to help the distraught leader.

When an empathic leader is arguing on behalf of others and he continues to do so even after others have tried to make it clear they disagree or that no change will occur, it can be seen as manipulative. Others assume the leader's intention is to wear them down through constant badgering. The perceived "whiny" protests are akin to a child trying to exhaust a parent into buying a coveted toy. The empathic leader will persist especially if his continued whining has resulted in the listener abandoning an opinion in the past. The feeling leader may be consciously or unconsciously aware of the manipulative nature of this technique.

Peers may also view a stronghearted leader as manipulative when he asks for help in placing an underperforming employee. The leader pleads a case for a poor performer, insisting the issue is a poor job fit. In the empathic leader's mind, he believes this to be true because he can remember a time when his role was not a perfect fit. Because the leader was identifying with the employee, he did not create any documentation of the employee's actual performance issues. The leader's boss feels pressured to find a new role for the individual. The boss assigns the employee to another leader, who will accurately assess the situation and determine if the employee is indeed a valued contributor or not. When the peer who agrees to give the employee a new position discovers that the issue actually is poor performance, the peer becomes angry. The colleague feels manipulated by the supersensitive leader into doing his dirty work. This peer must now prepare the proper performance documentation work and hold the difficult and uncomfortable negative feedback discussions with the employee. This builds resentment between the peer and the empathic leader. This peer broadcasts how the leader's oversensitivity has created extra work and extra risk for the company, solidifying the perception of the leader as being only concerned with his own needs.

The Case of Misty

Misty always went above and beyond for others, yet she would find coworkers distancing themselves from her. She didn't understand. She was kind, helpful, and a hard worker. She would share her personal or work challenges, figuring that everyone has to occasionally vent their frustrations. She thought this would prove her openness, build trust, and deepen relationships. At first her peers listened and shared helpful advice. This gave her the personal validation she so badly desired. When they shared their own stories of adversity or challenges, she would show empathy to their troubles by chiming in with a similar story. Eventually, the helpful advice she received from others started to dwindle. Relating her past experiences to their current misfortune started being perceived as Misty being self-centered or having an "all about me" attitude.

As a leader, Misty worked very hard to build a cohesive team where people enjoyed working with each other. She had a very caring relationship with her direct reports. They appreciated how much she knew about their likes and dislikes. They enjoyed that she took an interest in their personal lives. She would remember to encourage her team members who were involved in sports or whose kids were involved in events. On Monday mornings, she would ask about their weekend. She was also great at recognizing team accomplishments. Recently, however, her peers believed the recognitions were getting out of control. It seemed Misty's team was always leaving work to attend a celebratory luncheon. Her peers started complaining to the boss that her team was unavailable when needed due to extended lunches. Her boss thought some of the complaints were warranted but not all.

Several months later, Misty's boss asked for her help on a highly visible company project that was critical to a new customer. Her boss needed her to assign two of her team members to the project. Misty knew the project was going to last a full year and require members to work numerous nights and weekends. She was adamant that she could not afford to assign two members to the project. She argued that her team was already stretched thin and that losing two people to this project would severely crater the team. Her boss asked her to reprioritize her work and find a way to release the two employees. She countered stating that she knew the new project was going to take extensive work and all her employees had young kids. She didn't want to put that burden on them. Her boss replied that her peers had offered two people without any complaints. He added that the project lead was responsible for ensuring a proper work-life balance. He didn't want any more excuses, and she could consider it a direct order to assign two team members.

Her boss had been through this before with Misty, and he had lost his patience. He needed Misty to start taking a companywide perspective. Her focus seemed limited to only those she knew. In addition, he was tired of how much energy it took to convince Misty to think beyond her or her team's immediate needs. He had heard complaints from her internal customers that getting deliverables from Misty took too much effort and time. They complained that she acted as if every assignment was a major imposition to her team. In project meetings, she would include an emotional saga about how hard her team was working. When the work was finished, it seemed she wanted a medal rather than just a simple thank-you. They appreciated the high quality of work but felt she took too much time and energy to manage. He was starting to question her emotional maturity and ability to continue in a management position.

Misty was surprised when her boss provided this added feedback of the energy drain she created by complaining or seeking accolades for something her peers would have done without recognition. She was shocked that anyone would think her incapable of being a successful manager.

Getting Back in Balance

If you are empathic, please keep your big heart. Companies need your gifts to balance the left-brained leaders in the organization. Remember that these outcomes are not your intention; they are other people's perceptions.

Expand your empathy beyond yourself and your team to the greater needs of the organization. Consider what is best for the entire company as a whole rather than for a few employees. Your company is trying to meet the expectations of its customers, shareholders, employees, and board of directors. Apply your wonderful ability to see things from different perspectives to these constituents as well. Assume the intent of your company's leadership team is to keep the business thriving and to continue employment for its team members. Use your strength of empathy to envision the emotional complexity of everyone you have met and assume this diversity of dreams, needs, challenges, and fears is likewise represented in the company population. Include in this population all of the company leaders and investors.

Ask yourself before speaking if you are stating a case on behalf of the greater good or just a select few. If you can't speak on behalf of what is best for all and still feel the need to raise the concern, be certain to clarify that it only applies to a few individuals and provide clear reasons for your concern.

Use the language of the executive staff to make your points. Avoid using "I feel" statements. Instead, switch to "I think" or "I believe" declarations, and back them with data. Be careful of making statements that sound too much like opinions rather than facts.

You can practice this by listening to your voice and observing your body language as you recite some known facts, such as the multiplication table. Next, listen to your voice and observe your body language as you tell the story of your or a friend's recent misfortune. Notice how the first is clearly stated without embellishment and without assuming how another person perceives the event. Keep this tone and body language in mind when raising issues, such as the high possibility that the planned budget cuts will raise fears of future downsizing. It's simply a fact that based on your past experience this news will increase concerns of further cuts. Don't step into the employee's frame of reference. You can't possibly know exactly how each person will feel. You can only imagine, sympathize, or know how you would feel in a similar situation—but that is all about you, not them.

When the topic is about your opinion, your feelings, or your experience, be careful to match your words to the gravity or enthusiasm of the situation. Recognize that you feel at a much deeper level than most, so others may interpret your choice of wording as you experiencing something very different than you intended. Your sharing of a difficult situation may use descriptors that make others believe you require help to solve the dilemma. If you share too many stories of negative situations, this can unintentionally result in your being perceived as weaker since you apparently need more help. This is often not the case. You are just trying to have them understand how it felt to you. Likewise, when describing wonderful events, your wording may imply something miraculous. If their reality of the situation differs greatly, they will assume you often exaggerate.

One way to check if your response is a bit exaggerated is to look for overgeneralizations. If you are using inflated words, such as "always," "never," "everyone," or "the most," you can bet that you are a bit amped up. Check to see if any external factors, such as exhaustion or stress from another part of your life, might be clouding your judgment.

Be careful when describing an event or conversation that you are not describing another person as the wrongdoer, perpetrator, or antagonist. If you portray the other person as the offender and aggressor, you are unintentionally positioning yourself in the role of helpless victim. This is probably not the role you want to represent to your listeners. Ask yourself if you can be absolutely certain that the other person is intentionally preying on you. Chances are this is not the case. When you feel attacked, it is easy for that fight-or-flight response to launch a counterattack on the person you see as the aggressor. A barrage of slanderous bullets comes flying out. You might see the other person as "untrustworthy," "cruel," or "evil." You are now attaching negative generalizations about this individual's intention. Ironically, your behavior could now be seen as "cruel" or "evil." Both parties have no way of knowing with any certainty if the perceived intention of the other is true. You cannot know that this individual is trying to be your enemy. You cannot crawl into his head and find out. Therefore, you cannot know for certain that the other person is the aggressor and you are the victim. Instead, consider that you both have responsibility in any misunderstanding.

Recognize that there are times when it is better not to share your feelings and opinions. Consider the following questions to determine if you should say anything at all: "What do I hope will happen if I share this with someone else?" "What do I want this person to do other than agree or sympathize with me?" "Will talking about it change anything?"

Sometimes your only objective in sharing is to find a sympathetic ear or a sounding board so that you can sort out your thoughts from your feelings. This can be very helpful because as you listen to your words, you can sort through what is fact and what is emotion. The details you calmly discuss tend to be the objective facts, while the arguments that you spew forth emotionally are your natural defenses and counterattacks. But before you pop into your boss's office or your coworker's cubicle, think through who is the best person to have this conversation with. Is it someone at work or someone else? Would it be better to wait until the evening or to pick up the phone and speak to a friend who works a different job rather than to hit a coworker with a barrage of feelings that might be overheard or shared with others?

When you seek out that sounding board, make sure that you are not just seeking someone to agree that everything you describe is accurate. If that is the case, the reason you want to talk to others is personal validation. Be careful with this one. This is a temporary fix. No one but you can determine your worth. When the initial good feelings of having someone tell you what you were hoping to hear wears off, you will need to find another event to seek out this same validation. Recognize it is not one event or interaction that is leaving you questioning your self-worth. Feelings of not being "good enough" can be reversed but not with a single, feel-good conversation.

If after you exhaust the previous questions you still feel strongly that the issue needs to be voiced, then ask yourself two additional questions: "Is it even within the control of the person I am about to approach to make the change I am seeking?" If not, what exactly is your objective in speaking to this individual? You may find yourself back at seeking validation. "Is this issue best addressed by me or will it be more powerful coming from someone else, such as someone else on the team or a person with more positional power?" If you are the person who needs to raise the issue, take a deep breath and bring your brain out of fight-or-flight mode and up to calm, fact-based rationale. What are the undisputable facts of the situation? What are the perceptions held by others who are not as emotionally engaged? Be certain to voice these as interpretations of the event and not facts. What is the impact of the event to the company's revenue, legal risk, productivity, customer service, or other important measure of success?

If you want to talk about what is right or what is honorable, stop and reframe your conversation around the business issues of legal risk, impact to client relationships, or employee turnover. Likewise, your cause will be more readily heard if you quickly align it to the influence on quality or productivity rather than talking about employee engagement.

You have this wonderful ability to take other people's perspectives into consideration, so when you are preparing to make a case, use your gift to take the vantage point of your listeners and those you want to influence.

My intent in all this advice is not to tell you how to feel. Please take the time to acknowledge your feelings. No one can tell you not to feel something. Your feelings are a complex mix of past pain and pleasure experiences, beliefs that were formed to help you make sense of the world, and personal values that provide a framework for what is most important. No one else has had those exact same experiences, so it is difficult for anyone to truly know exactly how you feel. If you are looking for someone to validate your exact experience, recognize that this is impossible. Others can empathize and sympathize with you, but that is their limit.

To create lasting change, you will want to reprogram a few thought patterns that are unintentionally being reinforced and learn to validate and appreciate yourself. Use Part II of the book to help you with this. You are good enough, you just don't believe it yet.

GETTING BACK IN BALANCE REMINDERS

- **Take a Company Perspective:** Expand your empathy to the entire company and shareholders.

- **Monitor Your Tone and Body Language:** Check the tone of your voice and your nonverbals to ensure others hear your information as facts and not embellishments.

- **Match Your Words:** Be certain the choice of words matches the gravity or enthusiasm of the situation rather than how you might feel about it.

- **Eliminate Overgeneralizations:** Avoid using words such as "always," "never," "no one," and "the worst."

- **Avoid Casting Yourself as the Victim:** Be careful not to cast another person in the role of antagonist or perpetrator, which puts you, or the person you are defending, in the role of victim.

- **Know When to Share Your Opinion:** Ask yourself if this is the right topic or time to express your thoughts. Ask if the person you are addressing has the authority to solve the issue.

CHAPTER SEVEN

Visionary or Demanding

If you are working on something exciting that you really care about,
you don't have to be pushed. The vision pulls you.
—Steve Jobs, former CEO of Apple

Visionary leaders are the big-picture thinkers. They can quickly synthesize information, trends, and patterns to see what needs to be done next to reach a better future. They are great at getting others to look beyond the day-to-day outcomes and see the implications to the longer-term goals. This processing of information is not linear and often appears to jump to conclusions. However, when these visionaries unravel how they arrived at their deductions, others can appreciate their thoughtful analysis. Because they absorb information in large chunks, they see the world differently than those who analyze data one step at a time. It is the proverbial seeing the forest instead of the trees, and both views are needed for a company to be successful.

Being able to articulate a clear, compelling, realistic vision of a future with energy and excitement is important for rallying others to follow the charge. These skills are valuable whether gaining commitment to a project, designing a product, or enlisting others in the future direction of the company. These leaders do more than just talk about that future; they see it as if it has already happened. This imagery is compelling, and their brains can't help but work out scenarios of what actions need to happen now to reach that vision. Their gift enables them to see the steps needed, the consequences if the desired future is not realized, and the potential barriers that could thwart progress. As they crystalize this picture of the future, they become passionate about reaching this vision as quickly as possible.

Those working directly for these big-picture thinkers are thrilled to have a leader with a clear direction. They understand their purpose in the greater mission of the organization. This excitement, however, wanes quickly for direct reports whose preferred mode of processing information is different from their leader's methods. A big-picture leader starts with the image of the desired outcomes and deciphers the strategies and actions that need to be completed. However, the majority of individuals do not process information this way. These more linear thinkers start with the data and facts, determine the problems to be solved, and derive the actions needed to address those issues. These direct reports become concerned about the lack of analysis of the current situation to understand the gaps they are being asked to fix. They are waiting for a clearer connection to the here and now to chart their course to support the higher purpose. To them, there is a huge crevasse between the outcomes they are being asked to achieve and determining the precise roadmap to reaching that end point. The visionary mistakenly assumes that everyone processes information the same way he does. He can't fathom why some team members can't just figure out what they need to do to move forward. He expects the entire team to see the future with the same clarity and readily see the gaps that exist today. Team members, however, feel as if they have been abandoned in the forest without a map or compass to determine the way to the summit. These direct reports see their feet placed firmly on the ground while their leader's head is in the clouds.

The visionary leader misinterprets the need for more data as resistance. Not realizing that others are asking for a ground-level view, he makes the tactical mistake of repeating the same information only more intensely. When someone finally clarifies the informational needs, the visionary will recognize he needs to slow down and explain his analysis rather than just the conclusions.

As the visionary leader ponders the image of the desired end point, he adds visual details, sharpening the picture in his head. The juxtaposition between the conceptual image of where the project or organization is today and where it needs to be highlights the existing gaps. As these gaps get more defined, the leader becomes more anxious about the need to close these gaps quickly. Images of the risks of not moving forward ignite a fear of staying stagnant for too long. Soon this leader is no longer just enlisting others—he is insisting that others move forward to reach that destiny *now*. His words echo this fervor, and intended suggestions start sounding like demands.

"If we are going to reach this desired outcome, we *have to* move now!"

"We *can't* afford to wait! We *must* start today."

"If we *don't* take this initial step, then chaos will ensue."

Forget about the gentle nudge of "I would *suggest* we increase our efforts to reach the first phase," or "We *could* lose opportunities if we delay moving forward." This excited visual thinker is on a mission, and others are going with him whether they like it or not.

The leader's passion is at first contagious and then exhausting. Motivated to get to the end goal as quickly as possible, he works extra hours. This can send a message to others that they must also work with equal vigor. Combine this with the wording of "we must," "it is critical that we," and whatever other descriptors of urgency and importance come flying out of his mouth, and the feeling becomes the same—pressure.

When the leader applies this same pressure to those in more senior positions within the company, his efforts can backfire. His attempt at bringing others along on the journey doesn't feel like a pull; it feels like a push, a shove, and a heave. The listener is used to telling others what needs to be done, not having some visionary exuding revved-up energy forcefully stating what the executive needs to do. It's not surprising that the more senior executive responds to the perceived push by pushing back.

This executive has other priorities that weren't considered before the over enthused leader started rattling off what must be done. This executive may push back gently or send an indirect or direct message to back off. In this push-push interaction, the ultimate winner is the person with the hierarchical power. This will leave the visionary confused as to why the superior got so upset and lashed out to make a point. When it's time to give input on the future career path of this gifted visual thinker, the executive is going to remember the interaction and feelings of confrontation. Others who have experienced the same pressure join in the discussion. Quickly the conversation deteriorates to overgeneralizations of the individual not respecting positional power or having problems with authority.

Egotistical or Manipulative

When a supercharged visionary becomes singularly focused, he can become relentless in his quest to reach his vision. He doesn't seem to notice or care that other leaders have other goals. This can send a message that only the visionary leader's priorities are important. Other leaders try to share their focuses and workload, but the visionary doesn't seem to hear. Ironically, the usual big-picture focus has become narrowly defined to his scope of work. Continuing to push for progress on his goals alone solidifies the perception that he is overly self-centered or egotistical.

When this demanding leader does not get the action he is expecting from others, he interprets the resistance as being misguided. Refusing to take "no" or "later" as an answer to his request for assistance, the leader takes matters into his own hands. With conviction that his direction is what is best for the organization, he begins a clandestine operation to complete the initial steps required for achieving the outcome. When the involvement of others is essential, he will enlist them by stating only the short-term immediate action steps so as not to raise suspicions about the larger objectives. Later, when it is revealed that the work was part of a larger plan, those involved may feel manipulated. When the leader is told this, he is shocked that his efforts to help the corporation do the right thing would be seen as anything other than altruistic.

The Case of Alaya

Alaya could easily synthesize patterns and trends to paint a picture of how things needed to change. As she envisioned these changes, a full scenario of the future would emerge. Comparing the image of the existing situation with this image of the future enabled her to see what needed to change. This gift had gotten her noticed early in her career. She was brought into many special projects because this ability was valued and provided a necessary balance to the more data-driven perspectives. Her rosy picture of the future also made her enthusiastic about change, and this enthusiasm was contagious. The more she clarified the picture of the future in her mind, the more she became determined to reach it. This tenacity was appreciated, and her superiors knew they could direct Alaya toward a future need, and she would do everything required to get there. It was like pointing a missile toward a target.

In addition to her normal scope of responsibilities, Alaya was given special projects to lead. This expanded scope meant she was spending more time focused at the high level of each project. Her interactions with her team became more rushed. She assumed they could see what she could see and could figure out the rest. It was obvious to her what needed to be done, and she inferred this was the way everyone's brain processed information. Giving her team members additional information on the steps needed to reach the outcome seemed like micromanagement. This perceived lack of direction frustrated many of her direct reports, who were more comfortable with a sequential way of thinking. They would have preferred if she started with the facts and trends she was analyzing and then identified the problems to be fixed. Without this information, it felt as if Alaya expected them to read her mind. Her team wished she would articulate her full plan and not just the endpoint.

Alaya's broad perspective meant she missed conceptualizing all the details and tasks that had to happen to make her destiny come to fruition. Her concept of how much time it would take to complete each objective was overly ambitious. Having promised the executive team an aggressive time line, she exerted extra pressure on those taking care of all the details. Her intensity as a leader increased as deadlines approached. Her anxiousness over reaching the goal caused her to speak even more abruptly and forcefully. Her reminders about due dates became more like threats, which further increased the stress on her team. It seemed like Alaya had two modes of operation: the jovial, high-energy, creating-the-future leader and the intense, driving, stress-inducing execution leader.

Alaya's superiors experienced her in a similar fashion. They appreciated how much they could depend on her to figure out a direction and get things done, but her passion taken to excess was a bit much for them. Her normally excited demeanor became critical and demanding. She accused others of dragging their feet, not following through on commitments, or not comprehending the sense of urgency. When she felt rushed to reach the vision, she became parental in her language to her peers, telling them what they should be doing and how quickly they needed to respond. Since the negative intensity was temporary and often did achieve results, it was frequently overlooked. Soon, however, the complaints of Alaya being overly demanding and not appreciating others' priorities and pressures became too commonplace. The CEO asked Alaya to learn to be more patient and not drive so hard. They needed her to recognize when she was pushing others without appreciating their priorities that also supported the company's mission. She needed to learn that her behavior was not encouraging others to help her any quicker. Alaya knew she needed to slow down to allow others to come along on the journey, but she also knew this new pace was going to clash with her sense of urgency.

Getting Back in Balance

If you can identify with being the visionary, please keep those wonderful gifts of seeing what needs to happen to achieve a better future. Your ability to maintain an enticing outlook where you saw yourself safe and happy was essential to you successfully overcoming your adversity. Once out of immediate danger you reframed the negatives as having eventual positive aspects. Seeing the gifts hidden in turmoil enabled you to rebound from hardship. However, this ease of reprogramming can also keep you from noticing that your past experience continues to drive you toward the next better future at a pace that is unrealistic for others.

Pace your enthusiasm and sense of urgency. Recognize you are no longer in a fight-or-flight situation, and steady your expectations. You are most likely not in a race to save the planet from a meteor. Balance your need to reach that future today with all the other priorities and initiatives of those you are trying to enlist in your quest.

If you are the one in charge and can eliminate or delay all those other priorities so that people can focus only on your vision and aligned actions, then charge forward. However, remember that you need those involved to be committed for the duration. Beyond the initial burst of energy from others to rally to the call to action, you also need their sustained commitment over a much longer time frame. Continuing to push them to trudge forward when they are exhausted will eventually create resistance.

If you are not the one in charge and need the support of peers and other stakeholders, recognize that you are probably not fully aware of all the expectations and pressures being put on those you are trying to persuade to move forward. If you put your intense tenacity to reach the end point into pushing these individuals harder, they will resist. If they are in positions of power, they will match your force with an equally and sometimes more robust force. This can make it feel like you are ramming your head into a brick wall.

When you run into a brick wall, your head, no matter how stubbornly strong, gets bloody. At first it might not sting too much, but if you keep storming the castle with your head as a battering ram, eventually you will notice that not only are you in pain, but you are also the only person experiencing this discomfort. While you've been busy strategizing new ramming methods, the leaders have fortified their castle in defense. Each attempt creates more damage for you. This is not the win-win strategy you were hoping for.

Be careful of condensing time based only on your time line. When you start to recognize that you are getting amped up about the vision and feel like there is so much to do and not enough time to do it—slow down and breathe. List all the tasks and actions coming to mind and take a more linear approach. Think of each step required to close the existing gaps. Picture all the added activities you didn't anticipate in the last project that might have put extra stress on your schedule or delayed your effort. Add these to your list. Consider the number of available hours people have once all the unrelated tasks, interruptions, and normal nonproductive time is factored in. Stop and picture all the competing priorities, the normal downtime spent trying to get on people's schedules, the complexity of the organization, the time needed to complete required administrative work, and so on. There are many small jumps in between the giant leaps you easily see. Adjust your mental time line and project plan accordingly.

Next, check your language to ensure it is aligned with a realistic time frame for the project. Are you using emotion-laden words to push people to action instead of first requesting their effort? Identify words that acknowledge their priorities and their time frame. Choose statements that welcome them into the circle rather than drag them into the ring with you. Take heed of statements like "It's critical we complete this now," "We must finish this immediately," or "If we don't do this now, these consequences will result in failure" showing up in your conversations. Others may interpret them as you assuming they are not as committed to the cause. Your behaviors may also be interpreted as you thinking they don't understand the urgency of the situation.

Chances are, as a visionary, you have been told more than once that you are impatient. Acknowledge when you start to feel anxious about attaining the vision. Notice when you begin to worry about the lack of urgency others might be displaying. Anxiousness and impatience are just symptoms of an underlying fear. Your brain has moved back into its survival mode.

To identify the fears connected to this anxiety, brainstorm the following: "What am I worried will happen if the vision and tasks are not completed on time?" "How do I think these misses would affect the company?" "How do I think these misses might affect my performance and credibility?"

Keep challenging yourself to write additional responses to each question. When you have exhausted your list, identify the two or three that really concern you. Determine the probability of each of these outcomes happening. Identify the contingencies you could put in place to decrease the chance of these consequences if the probability is higher than you're comfortable with.

If being a visionary is your superpower, recognize that your gifts are not responsible for creating the friction you are feeling—it is your intensity in using them. Your foresight is greatly appreciated. Use those powers of visualization to see beyond your current scope of what is needed. See the fuller picture of priorities and challenges, and keep this broader picture in mind when engaging others. Remind yourself that you cannot control or foresee all the factors, and put some buffer into your time lines.

Chances are your overenthusiasm for the vision is causing you to condense time frames.

Your gift of vision is extremely important to your team and your company. Breathe into it, and you will get there just as fast and with a lot fewer bumps.

GETTING BACK IN BALANCE REMINDERS

- **Pace Yourself:** Balance the timing of your vision with all the other priorities of those you need to enlist in your change.
- **Set a More Realistic Cadence:** Consider the time it takes to get on people's schedules, complete all the administrative aspects, and deal with unforeseen contingencies before setting your project time line.
- **Avoid Verbally Pushing Others:** Check your language to eliminate words that imply you are asserting pressure on others to meet your self-imposed deadlines.
- **Manage Anxiety:** Notice when you are becoming anxious to reach your vision, and breathe. Assess your fears related to not moving fast enough, and determine which are based in past beliefs.

CHAPTER EIGHT

Highly Analytic or Uncaring

The most confused we ever get is when we're trying to convince our heads of something our heart knows is a lie.
—Karen Marie Moning, American author of the
Fever series and Highlander novels

Highly analytic leaders rely on their strength of sorting through facts, data, patterns, and possibilities to determine possible courses of action. From this information, they weigh the risks associated with each alternative, select one, and implement it. This enables them to come to decisions quickly and assuredly. They can even estimate the percentage of confidence they have in their proposed solution. These fact-processing leaders can make the hard but necessary decisions without hesitation. They can quickly cancel a project, fire a poor performer, sell off an unprofitable product line, or downsize the workforce as long as the facts indicate this is the best course of action. After all, they have thought through everything.

Well, not everything.

Their highly trained left-brain thinking has omitted an essential component of the analysis—the human factor. People have emotional responses. Customers care about products that are personal to them. Employees get passionate when a company moves their office space. Layoffs create fear, anger, and resentment. Direct reports seek emotional connection. Peers pursue relationships based on mutual respect. These feeling responses cannot be minimized without negative consequences.

When this superpower is overcharged, the perception is the leader makes these tough emotion-laden decisions in a very callous way. To observers, it may seem the leader didn't take the human reactions and needs into consideration. The leader might have thought about the people implications, but the amount of time spent on this part of the discussion is limited and doesn't explore the full ramifications of a potentially uncomfortable topic.

Although these highly analytic leaders can be portrayed as "heartless," "cold as ice," or as "a hard ass," they were emotionally connected earlier in their life. They were sensitive not only to their own feelings but to those around them. Their adversity experiences, however, taught them to hide this part of themselves for fear it would bring pain or ridicule. These individuals learned to toughen up and continued to do so based on these old beliefs. This could be from childhood experiences, but it could also be from experiences at any point in their lives. It is common to see women executives with this superpower. They had to fight their way up the career ladder and avoid being cast in the stereotyped role of an "overly emotional woman." Their adversity paved the way for women today to not have this outdated stereotype limit their careers.

Let me clarify that I am not describing leaders with limited ability to express emotion due to conditions such as Asperger's syndrome. Nor am I describing leaders incapable of empathizing with others, as is the case with psychopathy. Although these individuals are present in the workplace, the focus of this chapter is on those highly analytic leaders whose superpowers came from adversity.

Highly analytic leaders focus on the task at hand, what needs to be done, or what needs to be solved. Whether they start processing information based on data and details or start with a big-picture concept of the issue, they subconsciously eliminate the emotional aspects of the situation. These leaders are truly overly task focused as they have compartmentalized the relationship aspects of the situation to decrease their perceived vulnerability.

When interacting with their direct reports, these leaders take a straightforward and efficient approach. Issues are raised immediately and in a sterile manner. An employee's less-than-adequate work is called out without hesitation, sometimes in front of others. The facts of the deficit and the expectation that the person will correct the issues are stated without emotion. This is not personal—it is the work that is being addressed. To an employee who connects the work to personal value or who fears performance-review implications, though, the leader's response seems cold and harsh. The employee gets upset with the leader's insensitive approach. The individual does not share the view that the inadequacy of the work is separate from an accusation of deficiency. Other direct reports who have worked longer with the supercharged analytic thinker will seek to comfort their peer after the meeting. In an attempt to fill the emotional vacuum created by the leader, the caring peers will let the individual know not to take the feedback too hard; just correct the problem and the leader will be happy.

When providing recognition, the highly analytic leader will acknowledge when work has exceeded expectations. The praise will focus on the work itself. Gushing statements about the individual's efforts or capabilities will be noticeably missing.

"I want to recognize Sally and her team for their work on the scan project. This work met all the deadlines and the ambitious success measures. This new product will help the company move into the aerospace industry."

A less sterile recognition would have been, "I'm extremely impressed with Sally and her team's work on the scan project. Their creativity in finding a work-around solution to the t-pin problem enabled us to continue to meet the project deadlines even when it looked grim. The new features the team incorporated into the product exceeded both the executive staff's and customers' expectations. This team demonstrated the risk taking and tenacity needed to help us break into the aerospace industry. Sally and her team's expertise positioned the company for success."

Not only is the latter example more specific, it exudes pride and heartfelt appreciation.

It's not that these highly left-brained leaders don't recognize the role of each member in the work. Often these leaders would love to be more glowing and show more pride in the team, but fear keeps them from doing this. They dread that once they get started talking about how they really feel, they will emote too much and lose control of their stoic presence. Heaven forbid if they should gush with pride or glisten with tears of joy. This would be contrary to their hard-earned belief that emotions must be kept under careful guard.

Left unmentioned, team members feel inadequately recognized. Those direct reports who are themselves recovering highly analytics do their best to explain to others that the leader is more proud of them than it seems. This is a nice gesture but a poor substitute for the leader's heartfelt approval. Over time, some direct reports will tire of hearing excuses for the leader's behavior. These individuals will leave the group in search of a "more human" boss who can provide a more personalized connection.

When interacting with peers, highly analytic leaders can mistakenly see these interactions as purely transactional. They assume that their peers are as task driven as they are. They do not take the time to get to know their peers on a personal level. They don't make the time to go to lunch and learn what challenges a peer faces or how the work is negatively or positively affecting him. The leader remains focused only on the tasks and the support needed. This lack of relationship building and understanding of the peer's perspective can result in the peer believing the task-focused leader does not respect him and his scope of work.

At the senior leadership level, these highly efficient leaders are often asked to take on responsibilities that require the ability to make decisions that affect people's livelihoods. When the company is having financial difficulty and recognizes that the only way left to significantly reduce expenses is to cut overhead costs, these unemotional leaders can easily separate the personal consequences from the decision. Based on the facts and trends they see, these leaders can recommend reducing the employee population. They know that without these cuts, the company will continue in its downward spiral. They are well aware that their decisions will affect people's livelihoods and families, but they keep the possible emotional reactions of others at a safe distance.

When announcing the decision to conduct layoffs, they will acknowledge that this was a difficult choice because it affects employees personally. They will then share the logical reasons for the decision and the consequences to the business if this course is not followed. They will spend very little time on topics that deal with emotional aspects and spend the majority of the time discussing the logic and next steps. This is a mistake. They have underestimated the strength of the emotions that will surface from both those directly affected and those who work with those affected. These leaders' surprise at the resulting uproar of emotions is proof to others that they are "uncaring robots." These leaders may quickly find that many more employees are leaving the organization voluntarily than they expected or desired.

Egotistical or Manipulative

These highly analytic leaders are uncomfortable around displays of emotion. If an employee starts to cry, these leaders shift uncomfortably in their seat as their survival brains scream, "Run away!" These leaders will quickly summarize the conversation in order to bring the meeting to a close. This sends a message that a display of emotions is not appropriate. However, these leaders are certainly not devoid of emotion and can take things personally or complain loudly in protest of something they perceive as unfair. These impassioned responses can lead to a perception that emotions are okay for them but not for anyone else. Others assume this means these leaders are only focused on what is best for them. This can lead to assumptions that the leader is self-centered.

This egotistical perception is further heightened by these leaders' lack of effort in getting to know individuals on a personal basis. Leaders with this superpower view work as purely transactional. This creates a sterile exchange of work-related needs. These leaders' lack of warmth and connection reduces their peers' willingness to partner on projects or provide any discretionary support to tasks. There is no trust that these leaders will reciprocate the effort later.

These leaders can also be perceived as manipulative when it appears they are using other people's efforts to raise their own status within the organization. When these intensely nonemoting leaders fail to recognize others in ways that express genuine appreciation, those who feel undervalued start to resent these leaders. As they see these leaders receive heartfelt accolades from their superiors for the work their team or peers have contributed to, they assume that these leaders are getting the better half of the arrangement. It appears that these leaders are using the efforts of others to raise their own status within the organization. These highly analytic leaders would be shocked to hear these impressions, as they believe they have expressed appreciation of others' work.

The Case of Brad

Brad would have never guessed that he had a reputation of being insensitive or uncaring. Most of the time, his actions and decisions were met without resistance. Much of this quick acceptance was due to Brad's positional power as an operations leader. He had several factories under his direction. His immediate direct reports included managers of manufacturing, engineering, quality, and safety. Beneath this, he had numerous supervisors and team leaders. Brad had a reputation for sound analysis and decision making, so his verdicts were trusted. His group was used to taking orders and implementing them, and they rarely complained.

Brad routinely conducted site visits. He saw these as an opportunity to spot-check on operations and role-model interest and concern over production, quality, and safety. He liked that he could interact with those directly on the line and coach supervisors and team leaders. This made him feel that he was a very connected leader. His team saw these visits very differently; they dreaded them.

Brad would announce his plans to tour a factory one or two days in advance. His management team was required to clear the day's calendar to escort Brad on the tour. He did not want to give his managers too much notice so that he would see operations as they normally occurred. He did not want his team prepping the area or their employees for his site visits.

The day of his visit, Brad arrived by the company's private jet early in the morning. His team of managers met him at the executive airport with a van driver so they could conduct a briefing in the car on the way to the factory. As the team toured the facilities, Brad would look to his team to get his questions immediately answered. His managers took notes as Brad pointed out positive and negative observations so they could follow up with corrections or recognitions. After lunch, the management team would gather in the conference room to conduct operational reviews, troubleshoot, or determine strategic adjustments. Most times these meetings would last until seven at night. Brad thought this later end time was perfect. It allowed him to miss the heavy traffic to the airport. In Brad's mind, these site visits were highly effective and successful. He thought his visits brought the team closer.

In his team's perspective, these visits did increase camaraderie; however, the bonding was the result of venting their frustrations after Brad left. They resented his assumption that one or two days' notice was enough time for them to easily clear their calendars. They believed it showed a disrespect of their busy schedules and assumed their days were filled with routine. Asking them to meet him at the airport early in the morning and stay until seven didn't take into consideration their personal schedules. His planned "efficiencies" created issues in childcare, cancelled workouts at the gym, or missed after-school activities. Brad's walk-through of the factory always generated anxiety among the employees. His focus on the task meant every question was about the work. There wasn't any idle chitchat to build relationships or measure employee engagement. The employees felt they were being observed and evaluated. When Brad was done asking a group of employees questions, the respective manager would linger behind for a few seconds to smile and say a few words of thanks. This gesture would let the employees know their input was appreciated, and they didn't need to worry about trying to interpret whether Brad was happy with them or not. When Brad recognized a work team for excellent performance, he would say a few short sentences about the good job the employees were doing. It lacked the emotional aspects of warmth and pride. This left employees wondering if they impressed Brad or if somehow their efforts didn't quite meet what he was hoping to achieve. Brad's managers made notes during the tour of the employees he would recognize. The next day, the manager would go back to these employees and reinforce how much their effort meant to Brad and the company. They would elaborate on the company impact and add the missing heartfelt tone. The employees would beam with pride at having been recognized by one of the company's executives. Likewise, if Brad had chastised an area, the respective manager would address the employees the next day to ensure they heard the right message and didn't feel personally attacked. Brad's supposed efficient visits resulted in more work for the managers. They would joke that they needed to clear their calendars for two days—the first day for the visit and the second for the cleanup from the mess made on the first day. Brad's team was tired of playing buffer to Brad's task-focused approach. They were losing patience with the excuse that Brad's behavior was "just Brad being Brad."

When Brad was asked by his boss to do a 360-degree feedback assessment, his team gave him candid feedback. He was surprised by his negative scores in self-awareness, collaboration, and accepting feedback. He was also shocked by the candid comments about his site visits. Brad knew he wasn't a touchy-feely leader, but he hadn't realized he was seen as harsh and uncaring.

Getting Back in Balance

If this is your superpower, recognize that no one is asking you to make a drastic change or expecting you to suddenly be all warm and gooey or share your life story. Instead, you are being asked to build your awareness that work is based on relationships as well as tasks. Challenge your thought that focusing only on the task is efficient. It may appear that being task oriented is quicker, but, in actuality, it will take more time from either you or others on your team to get the results you want. In Brad's example, the way he conducted site visits seemed expedient. However, his site team of four managers had to exert a lot more time and effort the next day to compensate for his relationship shortcoming. In more volatile misunderstandings, it is the analytic leader who must spend the next day doing damage control, trying to explain his intention and smooth hurt feelings. Building relationships also saves time when asking others for assistance. It's similarly faster to implement a project if you understand a key stakeholder's challenges, hopes, and desires before you start. If you are a global leader, learning to be more relationship focused is essential to success in many cultures.

Here is the first simple concept that will require you to break some habits: *slow down to speed up.* By taking time to build relationships, you will find it easier to get support for change, garner help when you need it, and build a truly cohesive team.

One key way to build relationships is to break bread with others. Stop eating at your desk and go to lunch with one of your managers, a peer, or a key stakeholder. Schedule yourself for ninety minutes. Take the first thirty minutes of the lunch just getting to know one another. Ask about the person's family, hobbies, or recent vacations. When you transition to work-related topics, focus first on discovering the other person's views. What are her challenges and frustrations? What recent accomplishments make her most proud? What does she think of a recent direction the company is taking? Ask how your team's objectives affect her work either positively or negatively. Ask her opinion of how well your team interacts and works with her team. Learn more about her perspectives. This will also let her know that you are truly interested in listening to what she has to say. You will be amazed at the expanded view you gain from these meetings.

You are aware from my early story that this was one of my superpowers. I didn't figure out how impactful taking time for lunch with others was until much later in my career. I wish I had started doing it sooner. There is a misconception that you save time by eating lunch at your desk. There are days you may need to work through lunch, but if you are doing it on a routine basis, you are missing out on building strong relationships with others.

Here is another secret: the higher-level leaders you serve are usually very happy to go to lunch with you. They greatly appreciate someone taking the time to slow them down to learn their perspectives, hopes, and concerns. You gain insights and ideas you would have never been privy to eating at your desk. They don't mind investing the time to help you learn how to better meet their needs.

Next, challenge your self-image of being nonemotive. You have feelings, and I guarantee you show them. Think about a recent example when you were frustrated or angry. What did you say or do that demonstrated your emotion? Perhaps you rolled your eyes, made a sarcastic comment, or spouted a lengthy, highly analytic argument as to why your thinking on the matter was superior. Don't be fooled—you are emotional. Even if you don't think you are showing it, others know. They find ways to read you.

It is usually the heartfelt emotions like compassion, gratitude, appreciation, caring, sadness, and regret that you are most afraid to show. This is due to previous programming. Perhaps your subconscious is worried that some bully from years past is going to pop out of the wall and yell a derogatory comment about you being weak, a scaredy-cat, or a crybaby. Perhaps your subconscious is still seeking that "good boy" or "good girl" status you so desperately tried to earn by shoving your pain and hurt away and trying to act forty when you were fourteen. The next section of this book will help you uncover the source of the beliefs that are surfacing in your consciousness, but for now, know that your fear of emoting too much needs reprogramming.

Look at this faulty belief with your logical brain. Think back to a time when you have seen a powerful leader's eyes well up with tears. If you can't think of one, just access YouTube and type in "president cries," "prime minister cries," "queen cries," or "CEO cries." Watch the video snippets; they are very moving. Notice how no one in the audience sees the leader as weak. Instead, the viewers empathize even more with the leader and the message being shared. Emotions create a deep human connection.

I used to worry that if I told my team just how proud I was of their accomplishments, my emotions would boil to the surface and I would not be able to contain them. Finally, I asked myself what was the worst that could happen if I did share how I felt and emoted too much. The worst thing was they could see me cry. I figured that would either be horribly humiliating or they would finally know how much I care. I decided to let them hear and see what I really thought about a major achievement they'd made. I did my best to be heartfelt without gushing. At one point, my eyes welled with tears. This was my dreaded moment. No one snickered. No one found it inappropriate. They were ecstatic that their hard work was so deeply appreciated. So what is keeping you from saying and sharing how you really feel? Challenge any outdated thoughts preventing you from showing your team you care. If this image is making you squirm, revisit this advice after working through the book.

The ability to balance between the thinking and feeling side of the brain is one of the most important aspects of executive leadership. Leaders must be able to take the perspectives of others. If the leader cannot empathize with employees, customers, the public, or shareholders, it can result in public outcry and resignations. The inability to connect emotionally has led to the downfall of many CEOs. Too often their purely analytical decisions and justifications make the front-page news. Before you respond to a heated debate or an emotional outcry, stop. Take a few minutes to put yourself in the other person's perspective. Given her circumstances, life experiences, and beliefs, how would you see the situation? Make certain your answer takes this viewpoint into consideration. Being too quick to respond in a sensitive situation does not save time. It usually results in hours of the leader's time talking to people to undo the damage created by saying something that lacked empathy.

A trick I used when I was leading large-scale change was to picture the most sensitive or contentious individual I knew and think about how that person would respond to what I was getting ready to say. This always resulted in edits that made my talks much better and demonstrated that I could take multiple perspectives. If you find you are having trouble seeing something from a different vantage point, ask someone you respect who can easily assume that context to help you determine possible reactions. Ask the person how your message could be misconstrued. Ask what would make it better. If you find yourself wanting to justify your position, pause and start asking questions to better understand that person's interpretation of the message. Challenge yourself to really see the issue from another perspective instead of your own. It doesn't matter what you were trying to say—it matters what was heard.

GETTING BACK IN BALANCE REMINDERS

- **Slow Down to Speed Up:** Take the time to build relationships, and you'll find your tasks go smoother and require less course correction from you or others.

- **Schedule Lunch Away from the Office:** Spend time with those you want to build relationships with to learn about others' challenges, perspectives, and needs.

- **Risk Letting Your Heartfelt Emotions Show:** Dare to show how much you care and how it has affected you.

- **Consider Other Perspectives before Speaking:** Analyze the viewpoints of others and their possible reactions before delivering important communications.

CHAPTER NINE

Humble or Condescending

There is nothing enlightened about shrinking so that other people won't feel insecure around you. We are all meant to shine.
—Marianne Williamson, American spiritual teacher
and author, *A Return to Love*

It can be refreshing to find humble leaders. They serve as a needed departure from the leaders with an inflated sense of self. Humble leaders don't make the focus about them because they appreciate that they are only one part of a much bigger whole. These leaders acknowledge that each member of the team has different talents but see everyone as important to the overall outcome. They also recognize that they have different skills but view these as being no better than anyone else's in the organization. These unassuming leaders are careful not to bring additional attention to themselves and are modest in their contributions. Modest leaders like to be seen as true team players. They view their role as ensuring that members of the team have the resources needed to do their jobs.

There are many things others admire about these leaders. The team knows their leader is going to work as hard as they do and will not be above doing the necessary but unpleasant parts of a job. Team members are thrilled that the leader values their opinions and involves them in decision making. Peers are happy that the leader does not try to exert too much influence in discussions and ensures each person's voice is heard. The boss is happy there is at least one leader on the team who isn't overly focused on her own needs. Compared to peers, this leader can more easily understand when another department gets budget or staffing without arguing about it.

In contrast to many egocentric leaders, these leaders will take the time to get to know each direct report's career desires and provide opportunities for development. They will understand when people need to arrive late or leave early to attend to personal needs. They will still expect their team to meet deadlines and perform to expectations, but the pressure will feel less intense. Others will describe these leaders as friendly and laid-back. Team members assigned to them will be excited about working for someone who is inclusive.

However, when these leaders' humbleness is on overdrive, this honeymoon phase will be short-lived. In an attempt to create an egalitarian workplace, these leaders unintentionally devalue the hierarchical power within the organization. They embody the concept of equality by sacrificing their own status in order to be seen as a servant to their team, unknowingly devaluing their own positional power.

Ensuring the needs of each of their team members is met may seem like a worthy pursuit, but these leaders fail to foresee the times when the needs of each employee are in conflict with the needs of the organization. Decisions will have to be made that will disappoint and negatively affect others. Not every employee can take the same week off for vacation. Not every person can be assigned the most coveted assignment. Not everyone is going to be happy with the direction the company has chosen. In an attempt to please each person, these leaders reassess and possibly change direction every time a team member brings contrary information or offers a different course of action. These actions will earn these leaders the label of "wishy-washy." To team members, it will seem as if all plans are temporary, and they are standing on shifting sands.

The leaders who give away their positional power see the workplace through the eyes of their team members. When a decision comes down from the executive staff, they will interpret it in this frame of reference. They will apologize for the executives' strategic decision if it causes discomfort to their team. Initially, the direct reports will appreciate this identification with the group. Over time, however, they will wonder why their leader is unable to influence these decisions. They will question their leader's status in the organization and wish for a leader who could act as a stronger voice at the next level. The leader will be seen as weak and lacking confidence.

The self-effacing leaders' bosses will also lose patience with their inability to take a higher-level-management perspective. The expectation is for all leaders to present the company's direction with a personal endorsement, not diminish employees' confidence in the chosen course of action. Their bosses appreciate the inclusivity but want their leaders to remember that the company serves not only the needs of its employees but also the needs of the board of directors, the shareholders, and the greater community. Each of these stakeholders has a very different level of influence and power. This notion of disparate power will cause a subconscious conflict with these humble leaders' notion that all are equal. They will understand this at an intellectual level but be uncertain as to how they should act to serve each organizational partner and still be true to their core belief in equality.

During routine situations, these leaders' desire to be impartial is effective. A participative approach to decision making is welcomed, and people appreciate that every voice is heard. However, as stress begins to mount, employees turn to their leader to make a choice and set a direction. When an urgent response is needed, and the meek leader suggests the team gather to discuss alternatives, the team feels as if their house is on fire and they are being asked to sit in the kitchen for tea. The pressing situation calls for a quick, authoritative direction that confidently communicates, "Everyone follow me to safety!" Questions as to why their leader is not asserting her authority to make a decision begin to surface. Team members wonder how this leader got promoted when it seems obvious she is unwilling to assume the responsibility inherent in the position. The group begins to resent this leader whom they now label insecure.

This lack of confidence is not an issue of skill set. These overly humble leaders are often very knowledgeable and talented and have the experience needed to lead the team. Yet, in an effort to remain an equal, they don't allow these talents to rise to the surface. They fear that they will exert too much influence or make others feel less talented, but they can't hide their capability. Occasions arise where these leaders' abilities must be shared, and others watch in awe as they solve dilemmas, fix vexing problems, or offer brilliant solutions. As others publicly acknowledge these talents, these leaders do not smile broadly and say "Thank you." Instead, they drop their gaze and quickly try to dismiss the accolades with an "Aw shucks, it wasn't anything." Somewhere in the past, they were taught that modesty is a virtue, not to brag or stand out, or that they are no better than anyone else. Years of acting on this belief have suppressed any notion that their intellects and abilities are any different from anyone else's.

Devaluing accomplishments backfires in several ways. First, when others ask these leaders to explain further how they came to a decision, solved a problem, or accomplished a task, these leaders can lose patience. In their minds, anyone could have done this. They don't understand that they have an advantage. Their tone and nonverbals express a confused impatience with having to further explain something that everyone obviously already knows. This comes across as "Come on, folks, this isn't rocket science!" This makes these leaders appear as if they believe they are superior. Others start to conclude that these leaders know they are better and are trying to make peers feel inferior. The assumption is made that these leaders become impatient because they actually do believe others are less intelligent or able. Their attempt to position themselves as equals backfires, and they are now seen as arrogant.

The second way their humbleness is misinterpreted is when these leaders gushingly recognize individuals for completing a feat less than what the leader has accomplished. The employee knows his talented leader wouldn't accept gratitude for this level of effort and starts to question why his leader is being so appreciative of something she could have easily achieved. The person being recognized discredits the humble leader's seemingly heartfelt appreciation and assumes she is being patronizing.

Egotistical or Manipulative

As the label of condescending continues to grow in the organization, people will become increasingly suspicious about the leader's intention. The leader's nonassertive tone and choice of words emphasizing she is no better than anyone else will be heard as pretentious. Rumors that the leader is secretly egotistical will surface, and others will say the leader is feigning equality. Soon eyes start to roll in disbelief when the leader continues to discredit her worth to the organization.

Suspicions of manipulation will be cast as others wonder what motivates this leader to sacrifice her status and power to serve others. They question why the leader is so quick to minimize her authority when it could bring her, their team, and the organization advantages. Perhaps she is acting like a martyr to avoid the extra work that comes with accepting responsibility. Perhaps the leader hopes that if she stays in the background someone else will come forward to take on more of the burden.

When the leader's boss asks for a volunteer to lead an important project, this self-effacing leader hesitates. While the boss is waiting for someone to step up and assume responsibility, the humble leader is busy questioning if it would seem too bold to assume she has the knowledge and skills to lead the effort. She doesn't want to presume she is more suited to the job than her colleagues. She would prefer the boss ask her directly to take the lead. All this time spent in internal debate results in a peer volunteering to lead the project. As this scenario reoccurs, peers notice they are taking on more work. The leader's colleagues begin to assume this avoidance is purposeful and cleverly manipulative. The leader would be shocked that anyone could think she could be so conniving when she is just trying to be modest.

The Case of George

George was a manager who hoped to be worthy of a promotion to the senior-manager level. His boss had asked him last year if he was interested in moving up, and George told him he was very excited at the prospect. George was getting anxious for the company to invest in his development to help him prepare for the next level. He wanted to ask when this opportunity would start but didn't want to bother his boss like some of his peers. He figured when the time was right, it would happen.

George saw himself as a gentle facilitator to his team. He was extremely bright and skilled but viewed himself as no more intelligent than anyone else. He believed that everyone had gifts, and his were neither better nor worse. George would synthesize information lightning fast, calculate the implications, and determine the exact path leading to success. He was unaware that very few people could process data in this way; therefore, he couldn't understand how others could not come to the same conclusion as quickly as he had. Externally, he tried to keep a calm demeanor, but internally, he was losing patience with the plodding pace of decision making. He did not understand why others could not keep up with his thinking. His brain chatter would produce a judgment that others were not as smart, but his equalitarian beliefs would counter and remind him to be a better servant. When questions surfaced, he assumed he was not explaining himself clearly. In a calm demeanor, he'd respond, "No problem. Let me see if I can't explain it better."

Others were awed by his thought processes and knew they couldn't analyze as quickly as George. Their method would take many more steps and a lot more effort. George believed his ability to come to a conclusion was no big deal, so he would readily dismiss any accolades. He would even comment that anyone could do it if they just tried. When George made these comments, others interpreted it as George telling them they were stupid. George couldn't understand why someone might see this as condescending.

When making decisions with his team, George loved using consensus. This gave everyone an opportunity to contribute to the discussion. Since everyone seemed to agree about the direction they were going in, he thought there would be more team camaraderie. However, when the problem they were trying to solve was more complex, George questioned if his participative approach was beneficial. At times, his team's recommended approaches were missing critical information. He would try to steer the group toward a more practical solution by emphasizing some of the factors requiring consideration. Sometimes this tactic would work, but other times it would fail. He would finally lose his patience and dictate the decision he knew needed to happen. Afterward, he felt guilty that he had not been more nurturing of the team. His team confided in each other their confusion with his decision-making style. One day, he was very friendly and collaborative, and the next day, it seemed he would revert to an authoritarian method. When George popped into his more commanding mode, it appeared as if their leader's self-effacing approach was a sham. They knew George meant well, so they gave him the benefit of the doubt, but they wished he would be more consistent.

George's peers described him as a supportive team player with a hidden fuse. George was helpful and willing to lend anyone a hand. However, there were times when it seemed he lost all self-control and would suddenly become adamant that his way was the best way. George was not surprised to hear this feedback. Sometimes he felt that he gave, gave, gave, but no one reciprocated. He believed it was honorable to defer his needs for the needs of the entire organization, but his peers didn't play by the same rules. He didn't see them sacrificing their needs. Too often he felt that they took the prized projects and resources and he got whatever was left over. He could acquiesce to others for a while, but then he would start to get irate and finally assert his needs with too much emphasis. His peers were aghast at how this meek leader could all of a sudden become domineering. At first it was attributed to too much work stress, but when it happened with more frequency, they wondered if his attempt to be saintlike was just too much for any person to handle.

George's boss thought highly of him. She knew he could be counted on to do whatever was needed. She also believed he had the potential to move up in the company if he could learn to be more confident when interacting with the executive staff. She was worried his humbleness made him weak. When George was given this feedback, he explained that he didn't want to appear overly opinionated. He hated when leaders were insistent on their beliefs, and he thought it better to remain open to ideas. The best notions came from listening to input from others and then determining if the original conclusion needed altering. He hated when leaders were overly self-assured. He had ideas but wanted to hear from others.

In response, his boss tried to explain to George that the company expected leaders to set a direction. It didn't have to be a perfect direction but one George felt confident in. Waiting to gather all the information from every source just wasn't feasible for every decision. George's boss was concerned that he was not willing to assume the power inherent in leadership.

Although George talked about everyone being equal, he didn't always behave this way. Too often he took a subservient position and waited for direction and permission from the higher-level leaders to take action. His boss wanted George to realize he already had been given power to set direction and make decisions for his area of the business. George's boss was having a hard time trying to find training that would address these developmental areas.

Getting Back in Balance

Although well-intentioned, it's impossible to be perceived as an equal. People have different skill sets and types of intelligence, leaders have more power than employees, and owners have more power than leaders. If you have this superpower, your attempt not to exert more power than anyone else will be in constant conflict with the hierarchical structure of even the flattest organization.

When you competed for a leadership position, you had to convince others you could do a better job than your colleagues. You believed you could improve upon what had already been tried, and at a conscious or subconscious level, you knew that you were the right person to lead the team and the organization to a better future. All this takes a healthy dose of ego. This does not, however, make you egotistical. Leaders become egotistical when their motive switches from doing what is best for the organization to doing what is best for them. Because you already have a strong need to serve a higher purpose, you do not need to be overly concerned with becoming self-serving. Instead, you need to worry about being seen as having an overwhelming need to be liked.

Wanting to be liked by your followers has unintended consequences. It makes you hesitate when making hard decisions that affect your direct reports. It makes your direction sound too soft when you really mean to communicate a firm requirement. When your team fails to follow through with the sense of urgency you had hoped for, your frustration can shift from amiable to seemingly passive-aggressive. All of a sudden your gentle nudges have become a whack across the back of the head, leaving your team standing in dazed confusion.

Embrace the fact that you are not a friend to your team; you are their leader. They want you to provide structure and to buffer them from the stress and pressure you experience from your higher-ups. They want you to fight for resources so they can complete their work. Let them focus on their scope of work and not get distracted with how all the pieces fit together. You do not all have the same job. You are not equals.

Aristotle said, "The worst form of inequality is to try to make unequal things equal." I have several food allergies, including to sugars. My husband does not. It would be awful for me to insist he limit his diet to my same foods and never eat a dessert again. Likewise, it would be horrible to insist I eat desserts and put my body in pain. Either would seem cruel—but both are equal. There is a difference between treating people identically and treating people with respect, kindness, and honor. You can value each individual's differences, and you can say everyone's worth to the world is the same, but you cannot make them equal.

This can be hard to acknowledge if your adversity programming was built around overgeneralizations of inequality being unjust or if you were told no one is any better than anyone else at anything. Think about how you were unequal to your peers in school. Perhaps some subjects came easier for you. Perhaps you were athletic. Perhaps you were creative. If someone told you to squash your differences in order to appear the same as everyone else, you know the pain this caused. If you were told not to feel pride at a personal accomplishment because it would call attention to your advantages, you know the pain this caused. Ask yourself if you want to inflict that misery on someone else, and you will start to understand your team members' frustrations at you trying to be an equal, especially when you get the higher pay and bonuses.

Another common symptom of this superpower is the desire to solicit everyone's opinion on a decision. If you tell your team you are using consensus decision making, be absolutely clear you know what that means. True consensus decision making means that everyone must agree on the course of action. If agreement can't be reached, the status quo remains until consensus is achieved. However, there are many times when the pace of work does not allow for the current state to continue until a mutually agreeable decision can be reached. For example, fixing a broken piece of equipment that has stopped the production line or responding to a request for documents in a legal discovery by the deadline require immediate attention. Staying in status quo in these situations will have dire consequences.

This leads to a second problem—team members can feel very disempowered when the decision-making rules change midstream. You'll frustrate your team if you start by getting everyone's opinion but then decide to make the final decision yourself because you can't get agreement or because their opinions lack important information you possess. By starting with consensus, team members believe their opinions will count the same as everyone else's. When you abandon consensus and switch to being authoritative, your team will wonder what they did wrong or perceive you as manipulating them. They will assume that you knew what you wanted to do all along and just asked them for their opinions to try to get their support.

Chances are you don't really mean you want to use true consensus. Instead, what you are probably aiming for is consultative decision making. Consultative decision making is one of the best decision-making methods because it allows people to voice their opinions, but the leader has the final say on the direction chosen. It is still participative, but it clearly seats the power with the leader. Since by the nature of your role you are ultimately responsible and accountable, it makes sense that you should make the final decision. Your team will appreciate the clarity of the decision-making process and know they will still be given an opportunity to influence the decision. This is not to say there won't be times when you will use different decision-making approaches, such as authoritative, voting, or consensus, based on the urgency and amount of ownership needed. However, consultative is the strongest form of decision making if you want to involve others and not risk delay or remaining in the status quo. Since the leader is the one throat to choke if things go poorly, it is *fair* that the leader be the one responsible for the ultimate decision.

Make certain you own the authority placed on you when you were promoted into your leadership position. Too many humble leaders end up waiting for permission to do something that is already within their scope. Your boss is busy and doesn't have the time to know your areas as well as you. If you think something needs to happen, inform your boss instead of asking permission. Let your boss know what you want to do about it, how you will measure success, and how you will resource the project. He will tell you if he thinks you should do something different. Your boss wants to see you stand in your positional power and take initiative. Your boss trusts that you are not going to suggest something self-serving. Even if he tells you, "Not now," he knows your idea was born of the intention to do what is best for the organization.

Speak up to get your own needs met. Constantly considering your needs to be of less value than others' will result in you being perceived as a martyr. Some will begin to interpret your subservient approach as manipulative. Let people know when you need resources or support. There is no shame in asking for what you need to make the organization even better.

When others recognize your unique abilities, graciously embrace your strengths and say "Thank you." You are better at some things and others are better at other things. Expressing gratitude conveys that you are happy that others see the benefit you bring to the team. It also shows appreciation of the other person taking the time to recognize you. It is wonderful that individuals have different abilities. This requires us to work together and collaborate. Without these differences, we would not need each other.

If this is your superpower, recognize the impact you can have by owning the power both inherent in you and the power bestowed upon you as part of your leadership role in the organization. You do not need to be concerned that this power is going to make you egotistical. As you can see from this book, every superpower can be interpreted negatively. It is only when the leader's true motive is self-serving that it is egotistical.

Getting Back in Balance Reminders

- **Challenge Your Thinking on Treating Everyone Equally:** Instead, focus on continuing to treat others with respect and valuing their differences.

- **Use Consultative Decision Making:** Switch you primary mode of decision making from consensus to consultative when you are the one accountable for the outcome.

- **Be Comfortable with Your Confidence and Your Power:** Question if you need to ask for permission versus input when the work is within your scope of responsibility.

- **Ask for What You Need:** Speak up to get your needs met so that you can better support the organization as a whole.

- **Acknowledge Your Abilities and Say "Thank You":** When someone recognizes your contributions, even if personal in nature, acknowledge your abilities and his effort to show appreciation by saying "Thank you."

CHAPTER TEN

Precise or Rigid

Exactness and neatness in moderation is a virtue, but carried to extremes narrows the mind.
—François Fénelon, French author, theologian,
and Roman Catholic archbishop

Preciseness is needed for most occupations, particularly at the specialist level. Being exact ensures quality and avoids costly rework. Projects that are accurate to specifications increase customer satisfaction and avoid minor and major disasters. Determining the specific cause of problems, rather than just the symptoms, saves the company time and money. When a leader is meticulous, his boss is confident projects will be done to the exact terms required to meet the organization's or the customer's needs. As the precise employee is promoted, the boss is assured this new leader will necessitate the same systematic planning and accuracy from team members. The leader's team will have well-thought-out project plans, will execute to due dates, and will track their progress to success measures. If the leader is in a staff position, like legal or HR, the organization can rest assured the leader will know the laws, policies, guidelines, and requirements.

Direct reports appreciate these leaders' straightforward analysis and clearly defined views of the challenges ahead. Team members know their leader can be trusted to decide on the direction to take and will stick to this direction with steadfast determination. This makes it easy for the employees to learn from the leader. They are given a clear flowchart of steps with defined decision trees at each possible variable.

These attributes of precise leaders are highly valued by the organization. Their exactness is often highlighted as a shining example of the company's attention to detail and quality. Therefore, when their preciseness is on overdrive, it is often not immediately addressed. Initial complaints of these leaders being unyielding or rigid in their interpretation are quickly dismissed. These leaders' rigor saves the company time, reduces costs, and avoids legal risks. Only when there are enough complaints of these leaders' inflexibility resulting in lost time, increased cost, reduced productivity, or lost revenue will their bosses be able to see that their overuse needs to be addressed.

The boss may tell the highly precise leader to be "less black and white" or "less rigid." The leader is told to do a better job of analyzing situations from multiple viewpoints. He is asked to bring several alternatives and not just the *one* right option. Because the leader has been continuously reinforced for his rigor, these statements result in confusion. He wonders what the executive wants. He cannot understand how he could be doing anything wrong. He did what was required to assess the situation, ascertain the requirements, analyze the facts, and come to a solid conclusion. The boss's struggle to provide exact examples of past interactions or share how others view the leader further exacerbates confusion for this leader who likes things precisely stated. He assumes his boss is just reacting to hearsay.

This bewilderment is actually a symptom of the underlying strength of rigid leaders. They are wonderful at fact-based analytic thinking with strong cause and effect. Their struggle is with the more obscure feedback of patterns, impressions, and implications. They want something grounded in the here and now for solid footing, not something based on probabilities or possible future scenarios. Somewhere in their adversity, their unstable environment programmed in a high value for something tangibly concrete to adhere to. They trusted that if they followed these rules for success, they would be okay. This provided them a sense of control.

If the leader went to a traditional school, this notion of only one correct answer was further reinforced. Chances are the leader excelled at many of the traditional subjects and had little patience for those that sought out more than one possible interpretation. This individual is driven to find the one right, safe answer. Once the leader with this superpower has converged on his correct course of action, it will be difficult for others to convince him of an alternate possibility.

Direct reports become frustrated with this leader when their alternative analyses and solutions are not considered. This can be especially concerning to team members who are intuitive in their approach and assess the patterns, trends, and implications rather than the data and facts. These big-picture thinkers can see many alternatives to the problem and know that each will have some benefits and some drawbacks. To these thinkers, it appears the leader is converging on a solution prematurely. They also feel the leader discredits their more organic mode of analysis. Even team members who process information in the same step-by-step manner as the leader become frustrated when their recommended outcomes differ from the leader's and are dismissed. They feel unheard without an opportunity to defend their investigations. As these employees push back in support of their ideas, the decisive leader will reiterate his own analysis and stand fast that his answer is the correct one. He doesn't see this as being disempowering; he sees this as sharing the rules to success and ensuring the choice minimizes risk to the company. When this pattern of behavior becomes routine, employees will complain to the leader's boss, saying that their ideas are not being considered and that they feel thwarted in their ability to perform.

Peers and stakeholders want to be included in the decisions that affect them. They want to be consulted. This leader's attempt to save these individuals time or do them a favor by conducting the analysis on his own is not appreciated. Colleagues and superiors want the leader to involve them in the data-gathering phase so they can share a different point of view on the issue. When it is time to converge on a solution, they want the leader to provide options and the consequences of each recommendation so they can decide what is best for their area. This rigid leader's certainty in their opinion seems one-sided and unintentionally builds resentment.

The rigid leader's boss will also become irritated when the leader fails to see the "gray" in situations. When making decisions that affect employees, customers, or executives, there are many more variables that must be considered than the precise leader makes allowances for. Issues like experience, maturity, intention, length of service, or protected class can affect choices made about employees. Customer factors such as years of loyalty, speed of payments, purchasing quantity, and ease of doing business will affect the response. Internal factors such as politics, power, and personalities need to be considered when navigating executives. The boss doesn't mind explaining these factors, but when the uncompromising leader argues back at what the answer *should* be, the boss loses patience. The boss knows there is a huge difference between *should* be and *needs* to be for each particular circumstance. The leader will be seen as lacking the critical-thinking skills required to be effective at higher levels.

Egotistical or Manipulative

When these leaders become adamant that their chosen solution is the right one and argue with differing points of view, others can interpret these leaders as being egotistical. Their certainty in their opinion is interpreted as discrediting alternative analysis and thinking. To others, it appears these leaders are implying that they alone are wiser than everyone else. In response to disagreements, these leaders share their straightforward analysis, demonstrating how they arrived at their conclusions. This gets taken as further proof that these leaders are defensive. Others do not want these leaders to offer rationale; they want them to *listen* to rationale.

When a leader doesn't solicit others' input while gathering data or when the leader performs the analysis in isolation, it can be perceived as trying to control the factors and the outcome. Key stakeholders can get irritated if their views are not solicited. They interpret the leader's behaviors as trying to manipulate the final choice of direction. It will be presumed that the leader knew what he wanted to do all along, and the seclusion was purposeful to serve his own needs rather than the greater needs of the company.

These precise leaders would be surprised that their desire to find the best and right answer for the company could be misconstrued as anything but a desire to add value to the organization. They are perplexed as to how the same attribute that got them promoted could suddenly be so misunderstood.

The Case of Liz

Liz was an accomplished human resources specialist who was promoted to senior manager. She knew all the policies and company guidelines and was great at readily applying these to various situations. Her boss assigned Liz and her team to support one of the most demanding senior vice presidents in the company. He thought this executive, who frequently complained about human resources changing direction on a whim, would appreciate Liz's preciseness. Initially the arrangement worked. The executive was very happy with Liz's quick responses to his needs. Her by-the-book replies instilled confidence in the executive that human resources could be efficient.

Liz was contacted to arrange for the executive's administrative assistant's request for a leave of absence. Liz consulted the policies and told the leader exactly how much time she could have off and the requirements for eligibility. However, the admin was dealing with a particularly difficult issue with her son and needed more time off. Liz responded that the company could not guarantee her job if this was the case. The executive was upset at Liz's inflexibility and escalated the discussion to her boss.

Liz's boss called her into his office and suggested she consider other factors, such as the admin having been with the company since it started and the strong relationship between this individual and this very prominent executive. Liz didn't see how that had anything to do with the policy. She responded that the policy dictated that she handle the situation in a specific manner.

This was not the first time Liz's boss had experienced an executive escalating concerns over Liz's rigid interpretation of procedures. When she had been in charge of a companywide project team to determine the company dress code, he had heard she was inflexible and wouldn't listen to other people's arguments that were contrary to her view. She had tried to get the team to adopt a stringent list of what was acceptable and unacceptable. Others argued that if the company was going to be this strict, uniforms might as well be issued. Team members believed that Liz assumed the employees were incapable of common sense. They also believed that Liz devalued the team members and their opinions. The boss had to step in and get Liz to think about creating general guidelines that reflected the team's input rather than a firm policy. Once the team had agreed on the direction, members complained again when Liz spent weeks tweaking and retweaking the presentation to the executive staff. He told her it was more important that it was completed rather than being absolutely perfect. He explained that her continued revisions were not changing the essence of the proposal and therefore were not adding value.

When Liz's boss called her into his office, he knew it was going to be difficult for Liz to accept that the leave of absence for the admin needed to be more flexible. He started by giving her the feedback that the executive found her to be harsh and unyielding in this specific interaction. He asked her to consider the assistant's impressive years of service, the relationship with this politically positioned leader, and the personal circumstances of the request.

Liz stated that based on the policy, she was not willing to yield. She was concerned that if they made an exception for this individual, it would set a new precedent and others would ask for the extended leave with a guarantee their job would be held for them. Her boss asked her to think through the implications of her decision. He reminded her that she may be right from a policy perspective, but this was not just a logical decision—this was also an emotional one.

Liz continued to argue her point. Exasperated, her boss described exactly what needed to be done and told her to make it happen. She reluctantly yielded.

Several months later, during Liz's performance review, the boss tried to get Liz to see her pattern of behavior. She argued each example as a discrete incident with unique facts and circumstances. Her boss was losing patience with helping her see that the events were related to the same underlying need to get things to fit into neat boxes with clear rules. Liz was frustrated with the feedback and felt it was a personal attack. She did not understand how being "too black and white" could possibly mean not engaging or listening to others.

Getting Back in Balance

If this is your superpower, you may likewise be confused by the general feedback you have received. You may wish someone could give you a recipe to follow to help you determine what you should do differently. Unfortunately, that won't happen because each situation is slightly different.

Others are asking you to acknowledge that there are different possibilities or gray areas in each situation. Rather than think you have to find the one right answer, think of it as solving problems where there are multiple solutions and you should be able to provide a reasonable justification for each one. This may take some practice because traditional schooling has reinforced your thinking.

I recall watching *Sesame Street* with my kids, and there was this game they played where the song lyrics were something like, "One of these things isn't like the other. One of these things just doesn't belong. Can you tell which thing is not like the others before I finish this song?" There was a picture of a baseball, an American football, and a basketball. The "correct" answer was the football because it wasn't round. I would then pause the show and clarify, "That is only one answer. Tell me how either of the two other options could be the correct response." Take a minute and think about this example. How could the odd item be the baseball or the basketball? Use your creative mind.

It could be the basketball because both the baseball and football have stitching on their seams. It could be the baseball because the skins of the football and basketball are dimpled. I could provide my rationale to you, but if you have already decided there is only one right answer, you may not be able to hear me.

Let's try another one. There is a hammer, a saw, a shoe, and pliers. Which one is different? The obvious answer is the shoe because the other three are made for the hands. But couldn't it be the pliers? Think for a minute. How could it be the pliers?

The hammer, saw, and shoe only take one appendage to make them work, but the pliers take two. Try to find reasons why each of the other two items, the saw and the hammer, could be the odd item. This will increase your ability to see things from different perspectives.

Granted, I recognize if I were taking a test in school, my answers would not receive any credit with an unyielding teacher or on a standardized test. However, remind yourself that at work, there is rarely one right answer. There are only the better, more reasonable responses for situations, desired outcomes, and success measures.

Apply this same brain elasticity to a recent situation where you heard you were too rigid in your approach. Identify the alternatives that existed given the circumstances, politics, and players. Take the situation from each key participant's perspective. Identify in what ways they were justified to have this perspective. This will help you gain appreciation for a more organic approach to problem solving and help you hear others' rationale more easily.

When others challenge your thinking and your recommendations, your defensive brain chatter wants to prove you have the one right answer. Stop and ask yourself, "Can I be 100 percent certain that my answer is *the* one right answer for this circumstance, this individual, or this organization?" There are very few things that we can be 100 percent certain of, and one could argue that there isn't anything we can be so definitive about. Most responses are based on assumptions—the assumption that the sun will rise tomorrow, that the organization will exist next week, or that the same leaders will stay with the organization for the next three days. There is a high probability that these things will happen, but none of them are absolutes. Realizing this will open you up to further exploration of alternative opinions. You may still come to the same conclusion, but at least challenging your rightness will allow other viewpoints to be better heard.

This brings us to the next suggestion: when you do listen, paraphrase what you heard. Before you restate your opinion and decision, state what the others said so they know you listened and considered their viewpoints. Use words that demonstrate appreciation for their processing. This will help you eliminate the perception that you are unwilling to listen to contrary points of view. When stating your decision, instead of being adamant on your direction, show your willingness to consider new options if your concerns can be addressed. For example, "I understand you would prefer to go in this direction because of your past experience with x, y, and z. My concern is that this will set a precedent that could be very costly to the organization and put us in a position of legal risk. Unless we can find a way around these two issues, or we think the probability of being sued is extremely low, my decision is to continue along the current path."

Being steadfast in your opinion is important when you are in urgent or time-sensitive situations. These are moments when you should set a firm direction. However, when you are trying to get ownership from and support of others in your course of action, a bit more finesse is required. Ignoring the need to bring others along on the decision will result in having to backstep. This will take longer as you will need to rebuild trust. It is better to slow down in the direction setting than to back up in the implementation phase. This will also ensure you have not missed critical facts and information that others hold.

GETTING BACK IN BALANCE REMINDERS

- **Train Your Brain's Elasticity:** Approach problems with openness to *multiple* right solutions. Find opportunities to challenge your thinking to find several viable alternatives.

- **Support Others' Points of View:** Find rationale that could make other people's perspectives the correct perspective. It doesn't mean you have to agree with them. It just means you can support that they are valid points of view.

- **Challenge Your Own Certainty:** Ask yourself if you are 100 percent certain that your answer or approach is the very best for the situation, politics, and players. Recognize that your response is founded on assumptions based on your own experiences. Make certain you don't converge on an answer without exploring possibilities.

- **Let Others Know You Considered Their Point of View:** Paraphrase what you heard and what you acknowledge about their rationale so that others know you are not being obstinate in your own view.

- **Slow Down to Speed Up:** Gather others' input before determining the direction and approach so that you can consider other people's perspectives and data. Demonstrate respect of other perceptions to build the trust and respect needed for faster implementation.

CHAPTER ELEVEN

Great Listener or Lacking Confidence

When you talk, you are only repeating what you already know. But if you listen, you may learn something new.

—Fourteenth Dalai Lama,
Tibetan Buddhist spiritual leader

The art of listening is important for any leader to fully understand others and demonstrates that you are open to others' points of view. Listening takes more than hearing. It takes setting aside your own opinions and assumptions to consider those of others. It is an act that empowers the speaker and builds trust. People like great listeners because they receive a sense of validation that what they are thinking is worthy of consideration. It demonstrates a deep respect. This psychological reinforcement of the speaker results in increased trust and respect for the listener.

When a great listener speaks up to offer an opinion, others listen more intently. They expect that the ideas will be well thought out and will have already incorporated what was discussed. They know that this listener would not add something to the discussion unless he believed it would bring value. This can make the great listener's words powerful. Hearing others results in the listener being heard more intensely.

The leader who listens closely to her direct reports empowers team members and builds their confidence. Unlike other leaders, who may prematurely interrupt direct reports to redirect them toward the desired path, the attentive leader will gather the entire message to understand the employees' perspectives before channeling the conversation into a course of action. Taking the time to hear others rationale sets a more relaxed tone than the leader who is impatient to jump to action. The attentive listener provides a safe space for employees who are learning to become more confident in their thought processes. If the leader disagrees, the person is assured it was neither personal nor judgmental of his intelligence since his voice was carefully considered.

In a group setting with peers and stakeholders, the intense listener is often seen as the great synthesizer of information. She can hear what others miss and bring this to the attention of the group. If two people are making the same argument from different frames of reference, they can mistakenly believe that their views are in opposition. This leader can help them hear where they are in alignment of the same foundational principles. The talented listener is also able to paraphrase others' points of view in ways that dissenters can hear the logic of the argument. When the leader chooses to speak up in these situations, she plays the important role of facilitator. She is labeled collaborative, the peacekeeper, and is attributed with building strong relationships.

It seems the superpower of the great listener has little downside. Calvin Coolidge even once said, "No one ever lost his job by listening too much." However, this is not entirely true. Occasionally, there are those who lose their jobs for not being assertive enough. Even more frequently, individuals with this superpower stagnate their careers by listening too much. When their gift is on overdrive, their patience is seen as plodding and lacking a sense of urgency. Instead of the proverbial "all talk and no action," these leaders can suffer from "all hearing and no action." They can also be labeled as disinterested and uncaring when they fail to share their opinion in discussions. Leaders are expected to speak up and set a firm direction for others to follow. When these great listeners are perceived as hesitating to establish a clear course of action or allowing others to dictate direction, they are perceived as lacking the confidence to lead. These perceptions can result in an otherwise effective leader being cast to the bottom of the promotional and succession-planning roster.

Direct reports will become frustrated with their supercharged listener when they expect their leader to fight for their needs but, instead, she returns from the meeting offering validation for opposing points of view. The team becomes weary of taking an understanding stance about limited budgets, resources, or changes in direction. Employees begin to question if their leader has the fortitude to stand up to opposition. This group will also become dismayed when they need their leader to provide a firm direction and she turns to a more collaborative approach of seeking input from the team. This anxiety-producing situation will be seen as further evidence that their leader is weak. The team may talk among themselves about this leader's shortcomings but are often hesitant to raise the issue with the leader's boss. It's hard to complain about a leader who demonstrates a strong respect for employee contributions, especially when others in the organization complain about reporting to domineering leaders.

Peers also rarely complain about the great listener because of the airtime they receive for their own ideas. Frustration will mount, however, if a peer is looking for someone to further validate an opinion in order to sway the argument and the leader, who is assumed to agree, remains silent. Often this silence is the leader's survival programming of "don't speak unless you have something worthwhile to add." This rule for survival fails to take into account the tactical advantage of voicing agreement and reinforcing a position with similar thoughts.

Similarly, associates will become frustrated if they perceive there are two distinct possible courses of action and want people to choose sides in order to force a direction. If the receptive leader who appreciates the merits of both perspectives assumes a neutral stance, peers assume the leader is playing it safe. They further assume the leader lacks the fortitude to choose a course of action. During these two situations, colleagues will feel abandoned by the quiet leader. This contemplative leader would be surprised to learn that her normal rules of engagement are failing to provide the support needed to be seen as a team player.

The boss can likewise become frustrated with this leader when directly asking her for her opinion during a team meeting and she responds that she has nothing to add. This response tells the boss little. It is unclear what the leader initially thought or which argument she now considers most compelling. The boss wants to know that this leader could steadfastly choose a direction if she had no one else to consult. It appears that she just can't make up her mind or is attempting to escape accountability for the decision. Hearing from stakeholders and peers that the leader is overly quiet in meetings raises further concern that this listener lacks the strength and confidence to lead.

Egotistical or Manipulative

Most won't label these leaders as egotistical, since their behavior is such a contradiction to the stereotype of the brash, opinionated, self-focused leader. Instead, they are more often accused of being manipulative. Their reluctance to share their opinion can be interpreted as trying to gain a political advantage by watching the key decision makers' reactions to others' input to determine the most personally beneficial course of action. Their response of having nothing further to add to the conversation can be seen as feigning disinterest to avoid accountability if the decision does not yield the desired results. Their methodical approach to gathering opinions can be interpreted as purposely avoiding work and responsibility.

These leaders' motives can also be misconstrued when they acknowledge different frames of reference. Someone may believe that an immersed leader agrees with him as the leader listens intently and confirms understanding with head nods. A quick "I hadn't considered that; I can understand your argument" gets misinterpreted as reinforcing an idea. An innocent "I hear you" becomes distorted into a much stronger message of "I endorse this position." Because others pay deeper attention when these leaders speak, their brief comments take on unintended meaning. If their supportive acknowledgements are directed toward those in more influential roles, it is seen as brown-nosing or trying to gain advantage with these individuals.

Remaining silent when others need the leader to speak can escalate from causing irritation to outright conflict. If the leader has supported an opinion in a previous conversation, she may feel her voice has already been heard. If in a subsequent meeting others challenge the ideas and this leader does not speak up in support, the person proposing the ideas may feel abandoned or thrown under the bus. The person will assume the leader intentionally distanced herself from the controversy. This builds resentment and leads to distrust.

The Case of Alex

Alex was a well-liked manager. His team believed they had less drama in their workgroup than most of their colleagues who worked for more intense leaders. Alex seemed to have a natural ability to paraphrase team members' input in ways that helped the rest of the team stop formulating answers and more deeply consider opposing points of view. Alex was a natural mediator. The team also knew that Alex had their best interests at heart.

Most of the time, Alex felt his team was high performing, but sometimes they did not follow his directions as clearly as they should. Other times, he believed his team did not pick up on the sense of urgency that he was trying to communicate. In these instances, he wondered if his more easygoing style was ineffective. He'd become frustrated and lose patience when it seemed he couldn't communicate that his message was a clear expectation and not a suggestion. During these times, he appeared agitated, and his choice of words was harsh. Afterward, he felt guilty about losing control. This other side of him did not fit his ideal of an understanding leader.

Alex's peers and key stakeholders enjoyed having him serve on their special project teams because he brought a less frantic energy to the group. He had a reputation for calming down the highly opinionated leaders so different conclusions could be considered. He challenged the more vocal leaders to pause, suspend their thinking, and listen intensely to find merit in dissenting views. Others believed that the team's quality of decisions was greatly enhanced by having Alex present.

However, the downside of having Alex on a team was his seemingly unpredictable, intense disagreements in some conversations. In most, Alex would peacefully state his opinion. He'd patiently listen to others' input and then be swayed by strong logic to support another's view. Graciously acknowledging the thoughts of others, his actions would encourage dissenters to yield. Now and then, however, things would be very different. Alex would gently state his opinion, listen to others, and then calmly reemphasize the reasons his suggested direction was better. Then, as it appeared another idea from a less experienced but more vocal and persuasive leader was being supported, he would escalate his argument with agitation and anger. He would raise his voice, insisting he be heard and his ideas not be minimized. Others would turn to him with a shocked look, but they would listen.

Alex knew his oscillating behavior concerned his peers. Afterward, whether he won the argument or not, he felt horrible. It felt like the interactions were similar to a friendly, happy dog wagging its tail and playing with you one minute and then turning its head, growling, and snapping at you for no apparent reason the next. His peers seemed to shrug it off, assuming he was stressed over some work issue or having a bad day. Alex felt like he didn't know how to constructively get others to take him more seriously when he needed to be heard. He believed his usual quiet facilitator approach undermined his expertise in situations where others should be turning to him for the answers.

Alex was also concerned about the impression his boss seemed to have of him. He wasn't asked to present to the executive team like some of his peers. When he talked to his boss about his interest in being considered for future promotions, the response was rather disappointing; his boss had answered that she would consider it. Alex didn't think his boss was going to advocate for him. He knew the endorsements would go to the more vocal leaders. Alex thought this was unfair because he firmly believed he could perform just as well at the next level. He was talented but didn't see the need to remind his boss about his capabilities.

Alex's boss confirmed this perception. She did not think Alex was ready for promotion. He wasn't strong enough in his opinions, didn't readily share in meetings, and seemed to shy away from debate. She didn't put him in front of executives because he had not proved his ability to stand firm on his beliefs without getting combative. She thought maybe he was just an introvert getting overshadowed in a company of extroverted leaders. If he could not learn to contribute more freely in discussions and increase his executive presence, he was going to remain at the managerial level.

Alex was angry at hearing this. He believed the company had too many leaders spouting their opinions and dragging meetings and decisions on much longer than needed. He didn't want to become like the attention-seeking leaders, who irritated him. He didn't voice this to his boss. Instead, he quietly thanked her for the feedback and left.

Getting Back in Balance

Let me start by clarifying that the attentive listener is not the same as someone who is introverted, as Alex's boss thought. Being introverted or extroverted describes how you process information and how you gain energy. Introverts process internally before speaking, whereas extroverts process their thoughts externally for others to hear. Introverts get energy from reflection and their internal world, while extroverts get energy from interacting with other people and the external world. Either introverts or extroverts can be vocal in meetings, but in general introverts will think through what they want to say before saying it, and extroverts will process their initial thoughts without much forethought. However, in the case of leaders with the great listener superpower like Alex, it is not a matter of introversion but of programming. The overuse, like the other superpowers, is a survival skill. These leaders could have been very talkative, gregarious children who processed their thoughts out loud but somewhere along the way they learned it was safer to listen and observe.

If you are a leader with this superpower, there are things you can do that go beyond the usual advice of "speak up more." The first connects to changing beliefs about your power. You are powerful. You do have experience and expertise, and your opinions do matter. You have something valuable to say, even if it's just agreeing with another person's thinking.

When you get to the section on challenging your beliefs, you will need to look at why you might feel subservient to others. For now, consider that you rose to your leadership position for valid reasons. Your company's endorsement of you has given you permission to have your voice heard. Think of all the reasons why your voice is just as important as your peers' and essential to the success of the company.

Your openness to others' ideas is wonderful, but be careful of being swayed by the most opinionated person in the room. She may have valid points, but be certain not to discredit your own too quickly. Discuss the merits of different points of view to ensure the best direction is adopted. A free banter of ideas should not be mistaken for conflict. Watch how your body responds when those in the room enter debate mode. If you feel a pit in your stomach, your muscles clenching, and your breath shortening, then you know your perception of the discussion is connected to your survival beliefs. For now, take a deep breath and remind yourself that a debate is a healthy exploration of alternatives. Relaxing into the discussion will enable you to determine which views you want to support and to more readily speak your endorsement.

When someone asks for your opinion, give it. Avoid saying things like "I have nothing further to add" or "I think the points have already been made." Those in the room want to hear your opinion in your words. Clarify how you weigh the options and which alternative you endorse, even if it is just quickly restating your own point of view. You don't have to be verbose. A quick "I agree with . . . for these reasons . . ." is sufficient. Remind yourself that by speaking up, you are communicating your interest in the subject and your willingness to take a position. This will keep you from being misconstrued as detached or avoiding responsibility.

When you have something important to say, use an opener that conveys that intensity and speaks to your confidence in your ideas. For example, "Based on my expertise, I believe . . . ," "I want to make it clear that this is an expectation with a firm deadline . . . ," or "As the expert in this subject, my recommendation is to . . ." Be sure to use words that acknowledge your power. Be careful of softening your message with passive phrases like "I feel . . . ," "My suggestion is . . . ," or "It might be better if we . . ."

There is an old saying that silence equals agreement. If you disagree with someone, even in part, clearly state your opposing view. You don't have to declare that you think he is wrong. You can still affirm that you have heard his argument by saying simply, "You make several valid points, but I see it differently" or "My opinion differs in a few of the concepts." Statements like these help others understand that you are validating their thoughts but hold an alternative viewpoint. Take the time to clearly state what you agree with and what you believe needs revising.

Like Alex, there is a tendency for leaders with this superpower to swing like a pendulum from being quiet and calm to being overly intense in stating their needs. This often leads to feelings of guilt. To avoid this, raise your general assertiveness level. Rather than go from passive to aggressive, make an agreement with yourself to demonstrate your confidence in yourself and your thinking. Think of all the reasons why you should be fearless in using your abilities and your voice. Think of all the reasons why it no longer serves you to make yourself invisible. Set a goal to speak up more in meetings to make your position known. When you start to do this, it may feel awkward and like you are talking too much. Don't worry that you will become one of the irritatingly verbose leaders because the odds of that happening are miniscule. Your goal is not to speak more to gain more airtime or prove your worthiness, intellect, or importance; it is purely to eliminate misunderstanding of your opinions and correct assumptions about the views you support.

Become very aware of your physical presence in meetings and what this might communicate about your power and confidence. If you find yourself trying to minimize your presence by slouching or taking a less conspicuous seat at the table, notice how this may be related to an unconscious desire to blend in to the surroundings. Choose a more powerful position in the room. Sit up straight and act engaged. Expand your chest. Physically stretch up instead of shrinking in your chair. Notice how that makes you feel more confident. This body language communicates that you know you are valued and belong at the table. Increasing your physical presence alone will send a stronger message that you believe in yourself. When you minimize yourself, you give permission to others to undervalue you.

As you start to make these changes, you will notice that you gain more respect and power without giving up your wonderful abilities to hear and value differing opinions. You'll also notice others commenting that you seem more engaged and confident.

GETTING BACK IN BALANCE REMINDERS

- **Own Your Voice:** Acknowledge that your company has given you authority to speak. Know that your voice is as important as others' at your level and that the organization benefits from your expertise.

- **Become Comfortable with Debate:** Beware of being swayed too quickly by others who have valid points in order to avoid what you might be interpreting as conflict. Stay open to others' ideas, but don't prematurely abandon your opinion. Take a few deep breaths and engage in the banter.

- **Use Verbiage That Conveys Confidence in Your Opinion:** Check your language to ensure you are not minimizing the power of your opinion. Use words that acknowledge your expertise and power.

- **Exude Confidence:** Make yourself noticeable in meetings through your physical presence. Allow your posture and body language to communicate your value and assuredness.

CHAPTER TWELVE

Calm Under Pressure or Apathetic

Be like the duck. Calm on the surface, but always paddling like the dickens underneath.

—Sir Michael Caine,
English actor, producer, and author

When people are under high levels of stress, they have difficulty thinking clearly and performing their best. Their anxiety gets in the way, and they overthink the situation or lose confidence. Leaders who are calm under pressure have the ability to shift the energy of all those involved in the event. While everyone else has begun to hyperventilate, their deep, serene breathing sends a message: "No problem, I've got this." Their need to remove the unhealthy tension in any situation helps others focus on constructive problem solving.

Likewise, when a team they are involved with begins to show signs of conflict, these composed leaders take the tension out of the situation. Using a quick problem-solving method, they direct the team in identifying the underlying source of the issue and separating it from the emotional triggers getting in the way of resolution. With calmer heads, team members quickly come to resolution.

Direct reports are thrilled to have leaders whose self-assuredness demonstrates they are worthy of following. Assumptions are made that they have a wealth of experience and have seen every imaginable situation. This builds an instant trust that others will learn a lot from them. As thorny problems are thrown at the team, these leaders quickly break down the insurmountable into manageable tasks and assign them like they are routine duties. If an employee stops by their office with concerns or fears, these leaders put the person swiftly at ease. They show them that whatever the issue is, it simply requires an initial first step followed by another until the resolution is reached. Their belief in the employee's ability to tackle anything teaches the individual tenacity and self-assuredness.

In peer groups, these unflappable leaders are a steady anchor as the urgent and critical issues of the business are discussed. In contrast to their peers, who talk excitedly from the adrenaline rush of a possible doom-and-gloom scenario, these leaders respond to the situation as if it was another typical day at work. Their boss appreciates their laid-back responses and knows these leaders can be relied on to get the job done no matter how difficult.

Being calm under pressure is an attribute highly desired by leadership teams selecting future executives. Companies certainly don't want anxious leaders who make judgment errors. Nor do they want stress carriers who wreak havoc with their contagious negativity. It seems odd then that this strength could become a detriment, yet when it is overused, it creates negative perceptions and stagnates careers.

In many situations, these leaders' even-keel demeanor can be misconstrued as detached and disinterested. For direct reports, this can send a message that their leader doesn't care about the effort or the outcome of their work. Team members who have worked hard to ensure a project is done well and on time hope their leader will acknowledge them with an enthusiastic response that mirrors their own pride and thrill at their success. These leaders' nonchalant responses get misinterpreted as them believing anyone could have accomplished the same result. Their unruffled demeanors can also result in too little pressure placed on the work group during times of high stress. Others involved in the situation may see the team's routine pacing as inappropriate to the urgency of the situation. This can make stakeholders nervous that strict requirements and tight deadlines will not be met. Soon, concerns about responding with more fervor are escalated to the next level.

When these leaders' verbal responses to a situation do not mirror a key stakeholder's level of intensity, problems can occur. For instance, the CEO may be breathing down a leader's neck about an issue. If this generates a response equivalent to "No worries. It's probably nothing. I'll check into it," the executive's anxiety escalates. The executive, expecting to hear "I'll research it right away and get back to you within the next two hours," might question if the leader can be trusted to treat the situation as serious. Distrust can escalate if the leader does not recognize the need to provide ongoing updates on progress because, in his mind, he is handling it. The CEO will urge the leader's boss to monitor the issue to ensure it is dealt with appropriately. The capable leader is surprised to find his boss questioning his plans, tracking his progress, and providing updates to the CEO on his work.

Likewise, leaders with this superpower may also fail to forewarn their bosses or key stakeholders of an impending problem. Their desire to manage issues without fanfare leads to this detrimental oversight. Although the issue may not seem major to these leaders, they have failed to consider the other person's perspective. Those that need to be informed often have different expertise and are being held accountable to even more senior players, such as the CEO, board of directors, or shareholders. The boss or stakeholder will become upset if one of these constituents informs them of an issue that they should have been forewarned about by these leaders.

When this attribute is a superpower, the projected calmness is just a cover for the immense self-pressure to keep things under control and maintain a state of calm. Under the surface, this seemingly laid-back leader is actually rapidly anticipating possibilities and formulating proactive responses to ensure a constant state of composure. There is a ton of mental work going on behind the scenes to create a sense of normalcy amid the chaos. The projection of a "no worries" attitude serves to keep things in perspective and as a personal reminder that this situation is not as bad as what the individual experienced in the past.

Egotistical or Manipulative

These calm-under-fire leaders' mismatches of emotional intensity can be perceived as portraying an air of superiority. Colleagues can misconstrue their "been there, done that" demeanors as the leaders wanting to be seen by higher-ups as more capable than their peers. They see these leaders as trying to act as if they are unaffected by stress or petty emotions. Soon, peers are complaining to one another that these easygoing leaders are purposely undermining their credibility by acting as if they personally have everything under control.

Peers and direct reports can also get upset with these leaders when they have worked together on a particularly challenging assignment. As the team receives accolades for their hard work, these superpowered leaders continue to act as if it did not take a lot of effort. The team doesn't want their efforts minimized and resents these leaders acting as if the outcomes and results were easily achieved. Assumptions are made that these leaders believe they are above the need for public recognition, and this reinforces their perceived arrogance. Likewise, when someone brings to light an error or omission on the part of one of these leaders, and it elicits a bland response, it can get misconstrued as the leader trivializing the miss. Others can be quick to portray this leader as a hypocrite who believes he is perfect.

In these leaders' efforts to have situations remain monotone, they emotionally underreact to not just work-related issues but also to personal issues. As direct reports and peers share emotional accounts of life challenges, these leaders' tones, body language, and words do not reflect the expected level of empathy. Their guarded containment creates the perception that they have no emotional concern for the plight of others and care only about their own experiences.

Manipulation is presumed when others believe one of these leaders purposely misled them. This can occur when, in their attempt to keep every situation as calm as possible, the leader minimizes the urgency of a situation. Others who proceeded as if the request were routine can come under attack by more senior leaders for not responding quickly. This can anger those involved, and they conclude that the leader deliberately withheld information to create agitation with the customer or higher leadership. When the confronted leader does not admit his oversight, it leads to accusations of the leader trying to further his own career. In most situations, the leader is unaware of the miscommunication because eliminating the tension of a situation has become an unconscious first step to any event.

The Case of Natasha

Natasha had been at her company for twenty years and had progressively moved up to the role of a senior director. She was extremely capable, and her division was well respected. Her senior vice president and other key stakeholders knew that Natasha could be depended on to complete any task without fanfare.

Natasha's team loved how she could put even the most stressful event into a calm perspective. When an executive was bearing down on the team to get a project done, she would tell the team to stop worrying about the entire project and instead focus on completing the task in front of them according to the time line. She reminded them of the three contingency days built into the project that she was certain they would not need. She recalled how the team had only missed one deadline in the past and how those circumstances were not present in the current situation. This reassurance allowed the team to breathe easy and focus on doing their best work. Her team and her stakeholders valued how Natasha could immediately get others to calm down and take a more reasonable perspective.

Nataha's team's only complaint was that they lacked recognition. It wasn't that Natasha didn't thank members for their work or tell someone she appreciated their skills. The problem was that Natasha was self-motivated and didn't require a lot of recognition. This led her to unintentionally block recognition from superiors. On complex issues that had her and her team staying long hours, Natasha would shrug off accolades as if there was no effort involved. For her team, this was a source of discontent. They had given up their evenings, family time, and weekends for weeks, and they wanted the praise from the executive staff. They believed they had earned it. They didn't feel that Natasha had the right to dismiss this acknowledgment on their behalf. It seemed she only thought about her own perspective instead of what this level of recognition would mean to them.

Natasha's performance feedback from her boss was positive. She was rated as extremely talented. She made significant contributions to the organization and was viewed as a key leader in the organization. She built great relationships with her stakeholders and peers. The only negative issue popping up on her reviews was a consistent pattern of not giving her boss or her internal customers enough warning on issues that might affect them. Her boss recounted one particular incident where she failed to notify him or any other executive that one of their key vendors was going to be one week late with a crucial part for an essential customer deliverable. When Natasha received the call from the vendor, she challenged the provider to find a possible solution to reduce the delay. After exhausting several potential options, Natasha recognized that there was no way to overcome the issue. She quickly gathered her managers together to discern a new approach to progress on the other project components while waiting on the part. They created an intricate solution that still enabled them to meet the required time frame. She was proud of her team and relieved the project wouldn't be delayed.

Natasha chose not to tell her boss about the delay since there was a valid solution. She didn't see the need to bother her boss or raise alarms when it was no longer an issue. Unbeknownst to her, the CEO of the supplier company had contacted their company's CEO to apologize for the delay and inconvenience to this major project. The CEO immediately called her senior vice president, upset that the executive had not informed him of the incident. He demanded to know how this delay was going to affect the customer, and he wanted an answer now.

Natasha's boss came storming into her office. He wanted to know why he hadn't heard anything about the issue with the vendor. Natasha calmly responded that she had it covered. This made her boss even more agitated. He told Natasha she was not considering the informational needs of others. Natasha provided the specific changes that would be made to ensure the project was not delayed. She told her boss she didn't want him worried about something that was no longer an issue. This convinced the boss that Natasha did not understand the ramifications of her desire to quietly handle everything. He wondered if her attempts to correct everything on her own were related to conflict avoidance because it seemed she did everything in her power to avoid any kind of emotional escalation. The CEO believed she was overly focused on her own span of control and disregarded the needs of others in the organization. Both assessments had some truth to them. Natasha did believe that keeping things at a steady state would avoid unnecessary upheaval, and she did try to keep everything within her influence in predictable, tight control.

Getting Back in Balance

If this is your superpower, recognize first that it is no longer your sole responsibility to create a nonstressful situation for others. Your intention to dissipate tension, anxiety, and conflict in situations is well intended but not always helpful. Tension serves a purpose. It motivates others to find solutions when none seem apparent. It drives people to finish tasks that would otherwise be avoided. Anxiety can be helpful in identifying possible undesired outcomes so that you and others can proactively plan alternate approaches. Likewise, conflict has advantages. Conflict helps identify when neither party has the perfect answer and enables a solution to be found that is better than the original options. Find examples from your own life where these benefits have been realized. Keep these in mind to challenge your old belief that you need to be the one responsible for returning things quickly to a nonturbulent state.

Observe when you are using phrases as a self-calming mechanism. These statements are said aloud, but the wording is actually meant more for you than others. Watch for comments such as "This is easy," "Piece of cake," "No problem," or "I've got this covered." Although you are subconsciously employing them to reassure yourself, they can unfortunately be misinterpreted as egotistical or demeaning. Others can perceive that you are claiming to be more capable or that only you can save the day. Take a few minutes to think of the phrases you used in recent high-pressure situations and challenge yourself to examine if they were meant more as reminders to yourself. If they were, then consider not vocalizing them next time; instead, keep them to yourself as a quiet reminder.

As an alternative to using these phrases, find a way to mirror the tone of the situation and group. Say a statement that reflects your understanding of the urgency or difficulty of the situation and the emotions connected to it. Acknowledge that doing this may be difficult because it admits feelings you may be trying to avoid. Saying "I recognize that the executive team is anxious to get this matter resolved quickly" is going to elicit a bit of anxiety. However, that is the point of empathy—to share in the feelings of others. Watch your body's responses, as your muscles will probably tense. Immediately take a deep breath to turn off the flight-or-fight response and then follow up with a statement that lets the person know you are moving into action. One choice is to mention the first steps you will take to resolve the issue. "My team and I will immediately get started determining the cause of the problem and get back to you by the end of the day with a status report." This is much more effective than a superhero stance of "No problem, we've got you covered."

When you discuss directives and assignments with your team, ensure you are telling them about the emotions of those involved in the project. If the executive team is perturbed, tell them. If the customer is irate, tell them. They need an accurate picture of the situation so they can be sensitive to possible impassioned responses. Be clear on the expected time line, speed of output, and quality. Let the tone of your voice convey the sense of urgency. Again, watch your physical response when sharing these feelings to become more aware of how these emotions affect you. Immediately after stating the situation with your team, shift into describing what you and your team will do to resolve the problem. This will quickly return your focus to the positive next steps.

Think "we" instead of "I" to avoid the error of not informing or involving others outside of your team who need to know or be involved in a task. Reprogram your self-talk so that any time your brain chatter starts to say something akin to "Relax, I have this covered," change it to "Relax, *we* have this covered." Then ask yourself who the "we" should be in this particular situation. Think up, down, and across the organization to identify those with a need to know or a need to be included. Consider the impact to the departments downstream from yours who will have to deal with any changes your team creates. It is rarely your exclusive burden to fix an organizational issue.

Be careful of dismissing recognition not just for yourself but also for others involved in the project. If someone else has taken the time and effort to acknowledge the contribution, the act of rejecting it can be interpreted as telling the person she was in error for thinking the effort was worth merit. Think back to when you gave someone praise and the individual was genuinely touched by the gesture. Now think of a time when you showed appreciation and it was dismissed. Consider how you felt in each circumstance. Understand that recognition is not just about the receiver; it's also about the sender. If you don't think your effort was worthy of praise, instead of responding that "it was nothing," say something like "I'm so glad you were pleased." This shifts the acknowledgment from being about your perceived effort. This is also a great opportunity to redirect the accolades to others. By simply adding something like "My team will be thrilled to hear this," you shift the recipient from yourself to others who would be comfortable accepting the heartfelt appreciation.

As with any of the superpowers, these recommendations will help change perceptions and start you on your path of change, but it is the next portion of this book that will help you make a lasting transformation.

GETTING BACK IN BALANCE REMINDERS

- **Acknowledge the Positives of Tension, Anxiety, and Conflict:** Remind yourself that each can increase productivity, creativity, and quality.

- **Avoid Voicing Self-Calming Phrases:** Eliminate comments that overstate confidence, and keep these reminders to yourself.

- **Share Both the Assignments and the Emotions:** When preparing others to assist on assignments, ensure they know not only the expected outcomes but also the current concerns and emotional state of those involved.

- **Think beyond Yourself:** Recognize that it is not your sole responsibility to fix the organization. Consider others who need to be informed and involved.

- **Appreciate Recognition:** Acknowledge others who give it by not dismissing it, and ensure you don't unintentionally block recognition that extends to others.

PART 3

Becoming the Insightful Leader

Looking behind, I am filled with gratitude. Looking forward, I am filled with vision. Looking upwards, I am filled with strength. Looking within, I discover peace.

—Quero Apache prayer

CHAPTER THIRTEEN

Looking Behind:
Your Source of Strength

Never let your past experiences harm your future. Your past can't be altered and your future doesn't deserve the punishment.
—Maya Angelou, American author, poet, and historian

Most readers can find at least one superpower that resonates with them. If you noticed that while you were reading the superpower chapters you could think of examples where you were a little like the negative descriptors of every superpower, don't fret. There are times when each of us is overly demanding, critical, the know-it-all, too nonchalant for the situation, or uncaring. This does not mean you have all ten superpowers. It only means you are human and more self-aware than most. Focus only on the superpower descriptions that completely resonate with you—the ones that when you read the positive description, you thought, "Yep, I'm incredibly talented at this," the ones whose negative descriptions made you sigh, "Dang, this is me. I was hoping no one would notice." These are your true superpowers.

If you didn't find your superpower among the ten, then use the knowledge you gained from reading the chapters to uncover what others are trying to tell you. Ask someone who will be brutally honest with you to describe how others see your strengths and weaknesses. Have this person attribute a few negative labels to your behavior. Let this person know it doesn't have to be her own opinion but perhaps words others have mentioned. Remind yourself that though the label provided may be far from your intention, it is an external judgment of your behaviors. Try some synonyms to further clarify what others are trying to tell you (e.g., "unfriendly" yields "cold," "aloof," "unemotional," and "uncaring"). Using a thesaurus might help. Then think about what could make you seem that way to others (e.g., overly task focused). Once you break it down, you will find your superpower. You may even find that you can more easily link your feedback to one of the ten superpowers by using a different synonym.

With your new awareness of your superpowers and the advice provided in the chapters, you may think you have all the insights you need to start changing yourself and the image you project. Unfortunately, if you start concentrating on changing right now, your efforts will only lead to temporary change. You will be focused on containing the overuse of your superpower and attempting to squash the undesirable behaviors. You may be successful for a short while, but eventually some stressor at work or at home will trigger your fight-or-flight response, and your survival brain will spring your greatest strength into action to save the day. With your new awareness, you'll quickly apologize and vow to more closely monitor your behavior. Then another trigger will occur, and your Hulk-like strength will burst forth again. At first, others might recognize how hard you are trying to change and not say anything. However, when they see the same overuse spew out again in a different situation, they will assume you cannot change. They will say things like, "I can see she is trying, but it is such a part of her, she can't help herself" or "He does really well until things get stressful and then BAM! he's back to the old version of himself."

I've worked with lots of leaders who have been down this frustrating path. Their bosses told them the behaviors they needed to change. They graciously accepted the feedback and vowed to do better. They were able to suppress their responses for a while, but it never felt natural. They described their efforts as "constantly monitoring their behavior," "sitting on their hands," "trying to act perfectly," or "biting their lips." They found it exhausting. Many felt as if they were losing their competitive edge because containing the negative aspects also meant containing the positive aspects of their superpower. One year later, many were told their efforts were appreciated, but the same negative behaviors needed further improvement. Frustrated, they started rationalizing that the feedback was due to a bad fit with company culture. They dusted off their résumés and left to find companies where their strengths would be better appreciated. This often yielded success for a year or two, but then they started hearing exactly the same feedback.

Awareness of the existence of the behavior is only the first step in change. The next-level work requires exploring the source of the behavior deep within the survival brain. Superpower behaviors are rooted in beliefs of what is safe and unsafe, what will yield success, and what will result in pain and death. Some of these beliefs continue to be helpful, such as "don't touch a hot stove," but others need to be challenged. These beliefs are resistant to compelling contradictory evidence because your brain has deemed them essential to future survival. These beliefs are acted on at a subconscious level, and they are locked behind your brain's firewalls—firewalls that don't want to be challenged.

Creating lasting behavioral change requires reprogramming this survival brain. This isn't going to be easy. It's going to be like trying to ferret out a repeating error in your computer. You need to determine how you got hacked and find the hidden code causing havoc, but since it is concealed behind firewalls meant to keep you safe, it's going to take some focused work. It will take the following steps:

1. Focus on one superpower.
2. Find your adversity.
3. Reprogram your survival beliefs.
4. Appreciate the past.

Be kind to yourself as you do this work. Explore each area with childlike curiosity, and stay the neutral observer. This is not the time to question why you didn't do something differently or beat yourself up for retaining what you logically know are outdated beliefs. Your survival brain is very different from your logical brain and is programmed with one goal—keep this body alive. It is primal and childlike. Consider the kindness, forgiveness, and love you give to a child or pet that is just doing his best to survive. You would never bring up some incident from eight years ago or even three months past and tell him he is responsible for not having known better. If your normally sweet pet scratches or bites you, you immediately consider that your pet felt threatened for some reason, and you try to determine what caused the threat or pain so you can remove it.

Use this same approach with yourself. You are not the same person you were at the time of your adversity. Your experience was limited compared to today. If you were under the age of twenty-five, your frontal lobe was not even fully developed. You didn't have the language skills and interpersonal awareness you have today. Give yourself a break.

To get started on the four steps, download the "Looking Behind Workbook" at www.theinsightfulleader.com/book-bonuses, or grab a notebook or journal. Make certain that you are prepared to handwrite your thoughts as you read through this section. Don't type your responses on a device. Handwriting is much more effective at connecting you with your heart, emotions, and intuition. Going old school is better than high-tech when dealing with the primitive brain.

Take your time working through this chapter. The four steps don't need to be completed in one sitting. Give yourself time for contemplation and for your subconscious to release new insights. If you rush too quickly through this work, assuming you can absorb everything by reading instead of doing, you'll revert to attempting to contain your behaviors rather than permanently changing them.

Step 1: Focus on One Superpower

To start cracking the code of your survival brain, focus on just one superpower. You can always come back to this part of the book to repeat the process with another superpower.

Think of your superpower and how it shows up for you currently. Visualize both the positive attributes of this strength and the negative attributes when it is on overdrive. Picture a recent example where a stressor resulted in you feeling as if you were not fully in control of your response. Totally unaware that the flight-or-fight response had been triggered, you didn't consciously notice the pounding heartbeat, the teeth clenching, or the breath moving into hyperventilation. You didn't notice that your mind was screaming ATTACK! You responded with force, and you saw other people react. Eyes got wide, and people leaned back to create physical distance. Perhaps your response created a counterattack from someone else who felt threatened. Maybe you were able to gain composure and get the situation under control. Maybe you apologized. When you left, you felt guilty, knowing it was not one of your best moments. Possibly you tried to rationalize that you were provoked, but you still felt this was not the shining example of the leader you wanted to be. Relive that experience for a moment. Identify the negative judgments you placed on others. Make note of how you might have distorted the situation.

My highly analytic superpower is my strongest and most resistant. Although I tried to contain it when I received my initial feedback of being "unfriendly," I hadn't completed the work necessary to actually change the behavior. When I thought about how this superpower's negative aspects showed up at work, I thought of two examples. The first was when I was attending a meeting where a decision needed to be made quickly. I believed the issues were straightforward and that logic dictated only one response. Most of the other leaders were in agreement. There was one leader who continued to weigh the pros and cons of the options and was, in my opinion, overly concerned with the possible reaction of a small customer base. I became agitated. Inside my head, my brain was yelling at him, "Suck it up! Get a backbone, and make a decision!" My external response to this person became curt as I stated the obvious and told him that we needed his response within the next few minutes. I rattled off all the logical reasons for him to agree with the rest of us as if he had not already heard our arguments. Others in the room heard my tone, my volume, and my choice of words and stared at me in surprise. Later, one leader told me she felt I was judging the individual as incompetent. I denied this accusation, but, secretly, I did judge the person as not having the strength to be a good leader. I knew as soon as I left the meeting that this was not one of my best moments, and I felt remorseful.

The second incident that came to mind as exhibiting less-than-stellar leadership was an interaction with a colleague. We were both being pressured by the executive staff to get a new automated system for performance management launched in time for the next review cycle. We had some minor data fields that needed changing, and I wanted to make certain that these were completed prior to launch. She didn't believe we had time to make the changes and still be able to get everyone trained on the system. She came into my office and, in a matter-of-fact tone, said, "The executives are breathing down my neck. I know we want to get everything perfect, but given our time line, that isn't possible. We can't let a few minor fields not being ready delay our planned launch date. Do you agree?" I basically bit her head off as my survival brain pulled out my superpower to attack. I spent ten minutes justifying my attempts to rectify the data fields. My points were valid, but the method of delivery left me knowing that the same information could have been delivered without the drama. There wasn't anything she said that I did not agree with. When I looked back on the situation, I recognized that at the time, my survival brain took her comments and twisted it into an attack on my strength of leadership. My survival brain responded as if she'd said, "The executives are breathing down my neck *for your inadequacies*. I know *you want to get everything perfect* but we don't have time for that. *You need to be willing to take a risk* and launch now. *Do you lack the backbone to move forward?*" My brain responded, "How dare this person insinuate that I'm weak! I'm not weak."

I know this is a huge exaggeration of what she said. We were under a lot of stress, and that extra pressure happened exactly when my survival brain was oversensitive to perceived attacks to the deeply held beliefs that fueled my superpower. Both of these experiences were driven by my conviction that any sign of weakness was not okay, including hesitating to make a decision. My adult brain knew this was illogical, but that didn't matter. The survival brain had hijacked the reasoning centers of my brain.

Think about your examples of your superpower's undesirable responses being triggered, and identify your own mind's chatter. Consider if you lashed out because you felt psychologically attacked. Perhaps you felt that someone was challenging your self-concept, your intelligence, your expertise, your positional power, or your honor. This will help you see just how connected your superpower is to deeply held survivor beliefs.

After you find these examples, take a deep breath and recognize that this was not a conscious response. Remind yourself that you are on a journey of change, and awareness is the first step.

Step 2: Find Your Adversity

As you read through the description of your superpower, you may have started making connections to an event in the past when it was a matter of survival to quickly develop your strengths. If so, that will help you get started on this next step. If you could not immediately connect to an adversity experience, your adult brain and mature emotional responses may be blocking you. There are many times when someone finds her superpower but then thinks, "I don't have an adversity experience. I had a wonderful childhood and was deeply loved by my parents. I was well liked at school, and my life seems easy compared to those of other people I know." The key to finding your adversity experience is to use your much younger self to ferret out what triggered your flight-or-fight response and programmed your superpower. This is not a competition of adversity experiences. Just because your adversity experience was not worthy of a heartrending book doesn't mean you should discredit it. It's about the survival brain's interpretation of the experience from your frame of reference at the time.

One leader swore he didn't have an adversity event and spoke of his loving parents, but as we started to probe what could have possibly set off the brain's fear, he recognized that his loving father unintentionally created very scary scenarios on a frequent basis. His father had experienced many losses and difficult times, which programmed him with very deeply held survival beliefs. Determined to spare his son from experiencing the same life, his dad provided constant reminders of what was required for success. Harrowing stories from his past were shared in vivid detail. Unknowingly, this leader's father was routinely telling personal ghost stories of evil lurking around every corner. The fear, anxiety, and shallow breathing were palpable. They were contagious. His son could visualize himself in these situations. He never wanted to experience any of these horrors, so his young brain subconsciously programmed survival messages for him. As an adult, he knew his dad loved him and was trying to keep him safe, but his childlike survival brain was determined to also protect him. It set up beliefs based on his father's history. His father's recounting of doom-and-gloom scenarios became the adversity experience.

If the memories of your adversity event are only coming from your adultlike logical brain, the survival beliefs will be much more difficult to find and change. It's important to let your mind go back to the perspective of the child or teen experiencing the event. Find an incident that made you fearful for your safety and survival. It's okay that today you might see it differently. It's the logic of the time you want to uncover.

Another leader had a mother who set unrealistically high standards for her. Her mom compared her to her classmates, children on television sitcoms, and children being praised for accomplishments in the newspaper. This leader felt there was nothing she could do to please her mother. One day, she was being compared to a girl in her class who got straight As and had won the county spelling bee. Her mom told her that she wished she had a daughter who could make her proud. She added that she knew her daughter was better than an average, ordinary girl. The leader's child mind interpreted this to mean that average was not okay; she would need to excel in all things. Every example she could think of where she was not the best was proof she was flawed and unworthy of love. Her survival brain, knowing that without love and affection the body would not be fed or nurtured, went into panic mode and set the belief that she had to be the perfect daughter to win her mother's affection. She had an unspoken fear that if she didn't prove her worth, she would be rejected, and her parents would offer her to others for adoption. This was the start of her high-results orientation. Nothing but 110 percent was good enough if she was going to be successful in life. With today's adult brain, she now knows her mother just wanted her to excel and was putting the same pressure on her that her own parents had imposed.

What is important about adversity examples is not the egregiousness of the event but the brain's interpretation of it. Whether the leader has experienced being locked in an attic without food for several days, raped by an uncle, ridiculed on social media, bullied by a classmate or taught scary life lessons by well-meaning parents, the developing brain only knows that the body is registering a life-threatening event, and rules for survival need to be established. Don't worry if at the time of the event there were some eerroneous assumptions or exaggerations made by adult standards. Remember that you lacked the adult reasoning and experience you possess today. Also be aware that you could only see the event from your eyes and your mind at that point in time. Likewise, don't be concerned if others interpreted the same event differently. You have some inherent traits that made your experience unique—not right or wrong, just different. Perhaps you had brothers or sisters who went through the same events. They heard and saw the same things but stored their rules differently. Every parent with more than one child knows that kids show up with their own personalities from the day they arrive in this world. One baby seeks out active interaction while another prefers to be quietly cuddled. One toddler is sensitive while the other is stubborn. One child is imaginative while the other is practical. You stored your experiences from your own framework.

To begin, start with whatever memory first comes to mind that is connected directly or indirectly to the examples of your superpower you identified in step 1. Find the cases that triggered your flight-or-fight response. As you identify your adversity, seek to find a few specific, detailed experiences instead of general circumstances.

When I started looking into my own need to stay analytical, be strong, and not show emotions, the first event that came to mind was not the experience at the dinner table at age six. It was a later memory. When I was nine, I contracted plantar warts on the bottoms of my feet. They grew deep into the soles, and it began to hurt to walk. I tried to be tough because I knew the consequences of complaining to my father. The pain got so bad that I timidly mentioned it to my mother. When she saw them, she told me to show them to my dad. He briefly looked at the approximately forty warts and told me it was nothing. They would go away on their own.

They didn't. Instead, they spread like peanut butter on hot toast. There were now hundreds. I was scared. I could hardly walk, and my worst fear was that I was going to have to have my feet removed. I had this image in my head from an old war movie of a medic pronouncing to a soldier that his infected feet needed to be amputated. The medic gave the soldier a knife to bite on and then lifted a hatchet high into the air. As he swung the hatchet down to meet the feet, there was a blood-curdling scream.

This theatrical memory left me in a constant state of panic, trying to decide if I dare complain to my father or wait and risk an ax hacking off my limbs. Luckily, my teacher noticed my pain and sent me to the nurse's office. The nurse called my mother and insisted they take me to a doctor. This raised a new panic. In my family, going to the doctor was not a good thing. No one went to the doctor, and if you did, "you better damn well have something wrong with you." Now my survival brain was praying that the doctor would find something wrong with me. I had to wait another week in a constant state of panic for the appointment, wondering if the doctor would chop off my feet or send me back to an enraged father for wasting time and money.

At the doctor's office, my survival brain just repeated, "Be strong. Don't let your emotions show. If you show you're in pain or scared, the doctor will think you are weak. Be tough."

As I recall this event, my flight-or-fight response is triggered. My heartbeat quickens. My breath shortens. My muscles tighten.

I finally took a deep breath when the doctor confirmed there was something wrong with me—in fact, the doctor took pictures to submit to a medical journal because he had never seen such a severe case. I also took a second deep breath when I learned there was a treatment that did not involve an ax. It was an excruciating scalpel procedure, but I was going to get to keep my feet. Later, when the doctor cut out the warts, I squeezed my mother's hand as tears of pain ran down my face. I did not sob, whine, or complain. I did my best to prove I was brave and strong.

When your memory elicits your fight-or-flight reaction, you will know that you have an adversity event. You will know that you are able to see the event from the same perspective as when you experienced it. For just that moment or two, you won't rationalize it with your adult brain. The axe in your story is a real threat. Reexperiencing the emotions is key to uncovering the root of your superpower beliefs.

Take yourself back to that experience, and put yourself into the role of victim. Set aside any natural defense of minimizing the event because your programmed beliefs are telling you to be the strong one, the capable one, or the one who can handle anything. Stop your adult brain from covering the pain with higher thinking, such as "The person was just doing his best." Identify the persecutor. This doesn't need to be one person. It could be a group. Consider the accomplices who could have intervened but didn't. Don't worry about the persecutor's intention. Just look at it from the viewpoint of the age you were at the time of the incident. Note the belief or set of beliefs that this event created. Write these in your workbook or journal.

Ask yourself if the belief that helped you survive this adversity event was preprogrammed by an earlier event. Let your mind wander to other experiences, reliving each to find your adversity and your coping behaviors. Keep exploring memories until you find the event that initiated the reoccurring survival response. Find your equivalent to the Sunday dinner. This initiating event isn't necessarily the worst experience but rather the one that first provided insight into rules to survive future events. Find the first time these same self-preserving thoughts resulted in avoiding further pain or alleviating fear.

Once you identify the earliest adversity event, you can start to appreciate the necessity of your survival belief and the brilliance of your superpower. It is absolutely amazing that you were able to process the event and find skills that were adultlike in that moment. To truly appreciate yourself, take the role of a neutral observer, and forget for a moment that this situation involved you. Picture a child or teen of the same age that you were whom you are familiar with today. Consider how most kids this age would act under the circumstances. Now consider what your opinion would be of a kid who was able to find your same solution and skills in order to cope. I'm betting you would be amazed at his maturity, her ability to find a solution, or his resilience. You would have a much better understanding of why he is wise beyond his years.

Now feel that same sense of awe, respect, and amazement for yourself. See yourself as that child or teen, and tell this part of you just how impressed and moved you are by the courage and spirit demonstrated at such a young age.

Stay in the observer perspective, and fast-forward twenty years. Imagine that this kid turned adult is now working where you work, but you are unaware of his past. You look at his superpower capabilities and are fascinated that his skills seem to be second nature. This person seems to have a natural-born talent. What is even more amazing is that he doesn't recognize his uncanny power. In fact, he tends to get impatient with others who can't see or do the same things as quickly he can. Little do you know that, unlike others you work with, this individual has had at least one additional decade of using and honing this skill.

Stop and appreciate these positive aspects of your adversity. You gained maturity, courage, and resilience early. You had years to refine your superpower—something that others don't learn until much later in life. This gave you an advantage over many for leadership and is responsible for making you who you are today. Continue to embrace these hard-earned gifts while you smooth the rough edges created by the overuse of a few key beliefs.

Step 3: Reprogram Your Survival Beliefs

Identifying your self-talk during recent superpower stress events and during past adversity events provides insight into how entrenched rules for survival become. It doesn't matter if someone else believes the person's thinking is faulty or can provide evidence to the contrary; the bearer of those beliefs will fight with all his might to maintain them. These extreme reactions are based on notions of preservation. Every person has seen the results when the survival brain launches a counterattack to a perceived assault on deeply held beliefs—rioting, hate crimes, war, and genocide. Those who try to help the individual see the error of his ways offer an intellectual counterargument. However, since the opponent does not share the exact same experiences, the views are dismissed as misguided and wrong. Observers are quick to label the person with the seemingly irrational, deep-seated beliefs as a zealot, extremist, or fanatic.

In a very similar method of programming, your superpower beliefs are locked behind your own firewall of protection. Luckily, however, you have a stronger desire to transform than the need to prove your doctrine correct. Your yearning to be a better leader, partner, parent, and person confirms there is a catalyst for change. Your willingness to question, examine, and reflect serves as proof of your commitment to not only change but also to better align your beliefs with more recent experiences.

Identify Your Beliefs

Reprogramming your views starts with identifying your key survival beliefs that arose from your adversity experiences. Previously you may have focused on a key set of thoughts you repeatedly used, but now you want to find all the tangential beliefs that accompany it and explore just how deeply they are rooted. Revisit those specific events you identified in step 2, and notice not only the primary vow keeping you safe but also those that served as more than guidelines.

In the two events I shared (the rage attack at the dinner table and the withholding of medical attention), I learned the following:

Don't show your emotions.

Whatever you do, don't cry.

You have to go it alone—no one is coming to save you.

Be strong.

It's not okay to show weakness.

Be the responsible one.

Make yourself as small and quiet as possible.

Try to stay invisible—if you aren't seen, you won't be the target.

Picture a better tomorrow, and chart a course to get there.

Be as perfect as possible—don't provide a reason for others to find fault.

Brainstorm your beliefs without censoring them. Keep writing possible responses until you can't think of any more. Assume these were your personal scripture for success.

Because these beliefs are held at such a core level, we tend to be drawn to things that reinforce our righteousness in our position. Something as simple as our favorite stories, TV shows, and subjects in school may have become our preferences because they mirrored our beliefs. As a child, my most-loved bedtime story was Walt Disney's version of *Cinderella*. I related to her adversity and how she adored animals. It gave me hope that someday a fairy godmother would notice my situation and make it better. Hope is powerful.

Likewise, in elementary school, my well-worn books were from *The Boxcar Children* original series. In these stories, four parentless children survive on their own in an old abandoned boxcar. They get what they need by scrounging items from the dump or repurposing found objects. Each child has strengths that help him or her survive and solve cool mysteries. I remember finding hope in their story that one day, when I was a teen, I would be able to run away and make a happy home for myself. Both of these authors' works echoed many of my same survival beliefs. They also honed my faith that there would be a better tomorrow. It's no wonder I read these books over and over.

See if this example brings some similar awareness of ways your brainstormed beliefs were reinforced. Also, challenge yourself to find similar ways your beliefs continue to affect your preferences today.

When the book *Twilight* came out, it seemed everyone was reading it, so I decided to give it a try. I didn't see what all the fanfare was about. I thought perhaps I was missing something, so I read the second book in the series. It infuriated me. I found the main character, Bella, to be annoying and weak. Rather than standing in confidence, she kept asking others if she was pretty. I could have lectured for twenty minutes on how irritating she was. My daughter-in-law, knowing my disgust with *Twilight*, suggested I read *The Hunger Games*, and I absolutely loved it. Katniss was my kind of hero: smart, resourceful, courageous, and independent. She was also stubborn and had a problem with authority. Now that I think about it, it was like looking into a mirror. She was everything I vowed to emulate. She possessed both the superpower strengths and overuses I could subconsciously relate to. My visceral response to these books had nothing to do with the talent of the authors and everything to do with my own psyche. At a deep level, I am jealous of Bella for her ability to demonstrate insecurity so openly. How dare she when I can't? The same belief about what constituted strength versus weakness that hooked me in the corporate conference room was likewise triggering me emotionally in my entertainment choices.

Identify similar examples in your life today. These will provide insight into your most resilient beliefs and how you unconsciously continue to reinforce them. Highlight the beliefs in your list that might be a little on the extreme side.

Challenge the Beliefs

Within your brainstormed list of beliefs are some that are held tightly and some where the mind has already questioned their validity. In many cases, time and experience have provided compelling contradictions. For example, I questioned my "stay invisible and stay quiet" belief when I kept missing out on opportunities at school. I was overlooked for parts in plays or student leadership because no one knew I was interested. That outcome became painful enough for me to challenge the value of staying transparent. As you review your list, you will likewise find a few that you have challenged. However, be careful not to let your analytic adult brain trick you into thinking you have completely discarded all aspects of these beliefs. There are some rules of survival that are still subconsciously driving your behavior today.

For each belief, start by assuming that it is still dictating your responses. Challenge yourself by asking, "In what ways is this belief still showing up for me today?" Your answers might surprise you.

I would have thought that I'd discarded my old beliefs of "Don't show your emotions," "Whatever you do, don't cry," and "Be strong." However, when I confront the first statement, "Don't show your emotions," I immediately recognize that this belief still dictates my responses. The example that pops into mind is receiving some medical news that should have left me, at the very least, feeling a bit sorry for myself. Instead, I immediately went to rationalizing how the news was just life changing, not life threatening. I justified that I should be grateful because other people across the globe are dealing with medical death sentences every day. I visualized all the kids I've seen at Disney with Make-a-Wish t-shirts who are enduring so much and seem to take it all in stride. I immediately got to work researching how to minimize the impacts and creating an action plan to achieve my picture of better health. I became stubborn, determined, analytical, visionary, and results oriented. I did not cry. I did not pity myself. Somewhere in my mind, it was okay to shed tears over a character in a movie or feel pity for a friend experiencing challenges, but not for me. This is a prime example of perpetuating the same abuse on myself that I learned so well from my dad's repeated statement of "Suck it up! If that's the worst thing that happens to you, you'll be lucky."

Years ago, I attended a retreat with Debbie Ford, the author of *The Dark Side of the Light Chasers: Reclaiming Your Power, Creativity, Brilliance, and Dreams.*[1] During her Shadow Process workshop, she held up a baby doll with a cute rubber head, hands, and feet and a cloth body, arms, and legs. She had her dressed in just a diaper. She said, "This is Baby Pretzel. Isn't she adorable? Look at how sweet and innocent she is. Don't you just want to hold her and tell her how special she is? She is open to all your loving statements." She paused and then added, "But instead you tell her she isn't good enough. You tell her she is stupid. You tell her she should have known better." At this point, Debbie took the baby doll's arms and legs and twisted them in different directions. "Why are you doing this to her?" Another long pause and then she asked, "Why are you doing this to you?"

The point was brilliantly made. This image pops into my head as I realize that I am still using the "Be strong" belief. I have to question why I continue to unconsciously abuse myself with the same faulty beliefs that were imposed on me earlier in my life. If it were a friend who had been given the same medical news, I would have treated her with love. I would not question why she was upset. Although the belief came from my past, I can't blame this current abuse on my parents. In this situation, I am both the victim and the perpetrator. It is not rational. It is the belief of a fanatic.

You may likewise find that although you are no longer dealing with the past adversity and persecutor, you have unconsciously perpetuated both the belief and the abuse. Review your list, and note which beliefs you are subconsciously still using today. Ask yourself if you have unconsciously become your own abuser. Make note of which of your beliefs are teetering on the edge of being fanatical. Going through this process will help you identify the triggers that explode these deeply held beliefs to the surface.

---

1. Debbie Ford, *Dark Side of the Light Chasers: Reclaiming Your Power, Creativity, Brilliance, and Dreams,* New York: Riverhead Books, 1998.

Reprogram the Beliefs

Now that you are aware of the source of adversity and the beliefs that trigger your superpower's overuse, you are ready to reprogram them. This is not a matter of just substituting one belief with a new one. The adult reaction is to attempt to discard the brain's old command or at least try to keep it from surfacing. However, you already learned that it could still dictate your behavior subconsciously.

It's also not helpful to completely throw out the belief because there are times when the rule is still applicable. "Be strong and don't cry" was helpful to remember when the CEO was chewing me out and I was trying to be perceived as professional. It was much better to calmly own the error and apologize rather than wallow in self-pity and embarrassment. However, the mantra was not helpful when it became a dogmatic response to every situation that involved any emotion.

Therefore, the goal is not to completely eliminate the belief. Instead, the objective of reprogramming is to let go of the self-destructive behaviors by adjusting the parameters surrounding the belief. Like your superpowers, it is an issue of moderation and applicability. Don't throw away the helpful aspects of your hard-earned beliefs. There are times when they are very appropriate and other times when they undermine your effectiveness, success, and happiness. Instead of looking back at a belief and thinking it is faulty, recognize that there are times when it is helpful and times when it does not serve your needs.

The problem with these beliefs is not the beliefs themselves but how they were programmed. The survival brain has stored adversity rules as applicable to all situations that might involve pain. Because they were established at such an early point in life, they got inputted as absolutes. Remember that the higher-thinking brain, which provides judgment and reason, had not finished developing. Therefore, your brain had no other choice but to store these beliefs in the midbrain if it was going to keep the tiny being attached to it alive. These beliefs joined some other helpful commands, such as "Never cross the street before looking in both directions." The algorithm for our survival beliefs became "If there is risk of emotional or physical pain, regardless of the source, this rule is to remain in effect for all time." My survival belief became the absolute "Always be strong. Never cry."

Today, if someone gave you a command that contained the descriptor "always" or "never," you would question its validity. Intellectually, you have learned that rarely is something certain in all cases. To remove the rule from the midbrain and bring it into the frontal cortex, attach conditional "if this, then that" statements to the belief. For example, *if* someone in a position of authority at work is chastising me, *then* not crying remains in effect. *If* my pet has died, *then* it is okay to cry and show emotion.

Review your brainstormed beliefs, and for each belief, identify an example of where it is still true today and a recent experience where it was not applicable. Prove to yourself that the belief is not an absolute. Find the differentiators that will allow you to reprogram the belief with conditional statements of "if this, then that." Use this recoding to pull your beliefs out from behind the protective firewall of the survival brain and into the realm of analysis of the frontal lobe.

In order to begin this process, start with your most deeply held survival belief stated in absolute terms. Write this old belief as a firm statement. For example, "Showing emotion is a sign of weakness." Make certain it lasers in on your deepest fear.

Next, identify the ways this absolute belief has resulted in negative outcomes at work, at home, and with friends. Use actual situations as data points. Perhaps your examples are of ways you limited your own happiness, were unkind to yourself or others, or experienced painful events. Attach feelings to these memories: regret, sadness, guilt, and so on. Also think about the ways this belief has been unkind to you. Again, attach emotion to these memories.

Third, think about how you unintentionally impose this belief on others. Identify the expectations and judgments that affect those at work, at home, or in your social life. Revisit your examples from step 1 to see how you impose your beliefs and fears onto others. Use these more recent experiences to think about the outcomes you unintentionally create.

Fourth, think about what you might have accomplished if this belief were not an absolute rule. Describe how loosening it would make your life better at work, at home, and in your social life.

Now, switch to thinking about how this same belief has protected you. Identify when it was to your advantage to have it at work, at home, and with friends. Once again, give specific examples for each experience.

Considering your overall analysis of when the belief has limited you as well as when it has served you, create the "if this, then that" statements that better fit the leader and person you wish to be. Take the time to clarify each statement, and capture these in your workbook or journal.

As your absolute beliefs turn into conditional statements, they move from survival doctrine into the logical brain. When situations occur that challenge the old dogma, you now approach them with curiosity instead of fear of being personally challenged. This enables you to reach the higher state of rationalization that you seek.

Step 4: Appreciate the Past

Before you can release the past, you need to acknowledge the strength, courage, and resilience it provided. If you don't recognize the purpose it served at that time in your life, you will fight to destroy it rather than reprogram it. Remember that the belief is not always wrong. There are times when it no longer serves your best interests and other times when it does. Years ago, it was essential to your self-preservation. It was based on your analysis of the situation at that time.

As you reprogrammed your beliefs, you may have triggered some guilt or shame and asked yourself why you didn't notice these mind games at play before now. It wasn't from not trying. Before picking up this book, you had already made great progress and become consciously aware of times when your behavior did not fit the image of the leader you had hoped to be. Think of all the leaders who are still unaware that their behavior is out of sync.

This may seem like I'm telling you to forgive yourself, but instead I'm asking you to accept yourself for who you were when your superpower was forged, who you've been as a leader, and who you are now becoming. Appreciate the journey. Forgiveness implies compassion. Compassion is defined as sympathy with a strong desire to alleviate the suffering of the person you are trying to forgive. However, pity and sympathy are just another form of judgment because they assume that the opinions and values held today are far superior. They imply that the person giving forgiveness has knowledge of what is best. They impose the person's current belief system on the individual he pities. This would mean you would evaluate your younger self within the judgments of your current self. The hidden assumption is that your past self needs healing from this suffering. This unintentionally keeps you in the role of victim and others in the role of persecutor. It perpetuates your drama.

Instead of forgiveness, focus on gratitude. Be grateful that you have come so far on your path. Be genuinely impressed with your ability to try different approaches to your stressful situations and to create guidelines for yourself given your capabilities in each circumstance. Remind yourself of the negative consequences that might have resulted if you had not been able to discern your rules for survival. Acknowledge the gift and resilience each belief brought to you. Take the time to think through what your life might have been like if you hadn't adopted these survival techniques. Be amazed with your brain's ability to create such a protective device.

Likewise, let go of any shame or guilt associated with more recent examples of acting on these beliefs. You were not as self-aware as you now are. These thoughts were based on your knowledge, tools, and experiences at the time. You wouldn't expect the scientists of yesteryear to hang their heads in shame because they thought the atom was the smallest particle of matter. They did the best with what they had, and they should feel proud they took the scientific journey as far as they did. Error comes from judgment, and judgment comes from evaluations. Humans are always evaluating what is safe, right, good, healthy, and in the best interests of both one's self and the collective whole.

Don't just give this appreciation a cursory thank-you. Think to yourself, "Thank you for keeping me safe. I acknowledge the wonderful gifts this belief has given to me. I credit this belief for making me who I am today. I appreciate its value at the time even if I no longer need to act on this belief today with such absolute certainty." This shift in perspective enables you to shed your story and move from being the victim to embracing the wonderful strengths of your superpower. It allows you to let go of the notion that your beliefs are absolutes rather than guidelines dependent on new circumstances. Write a statement of gratitude in your own words to acknowledge the positive impact your adversity and survival beliefs had on your life.

You can use this same technique of understanding without interjecting your own opinion and values to examine the behaviors of those previously placed in the role of persecutor. Seek only awareness. Don't worry that there is some action you need to take. When I adopt the role of neutral observer, I understand why my father, who had so many mental challenges, could not make any other choice but to be self-serving. I understand why my mother chose to escape into her cocktails and romance novels to create her own version of not being seen. This awareness allows me to view them not as purposeful persecutors. It permits me to consider the advantages that resulted from the adversity I experienced. Letting go of the evaluations I placed on others is calming. Releasing the drama of my story is freeing. However, I'm not a saint. I don't consistently stay in this higher state. Occasionally a memory gets triggered that takes me back to feelings of being the victim. This is an opportunity to explore the balance between my experiences, thoughts, observations, and insights.

Don't feel inferior if you slip back into judgment now and then. Remember that evaluation and judgment are the brain's constant programming to avoid painful and life-threatening situations. It's a fallacy that anyone can always stay in the neutral observer position and stop judgment completely. Telling yourself to suspend judgment is a judgment itself that you are not yet good enough. When an unconscious memory or belief is triggered, use the techniques in this chapter to gently guide your brain from the flight-or-fight response to the frontal lobe and then to the heart and higher self. Remind yourself that no one is asking you to be perfect. Instead be grateful for all the work you have accomplished to become a more insightful leader.

Look back at the work you have done; you have

- identified your superpower,
- explored the advantages of your superpower and the negative perceptions it creates when overused,
- discovered the adversity event that accelerated its development,
- uncovered the survival beliefs triggering your superpower's overuse,
- reprogrammed these beliefs from absolutes to conditional algorithms, and
- reconsidered how you define your past and your present.

The journey to become an insightful leader requires traveling a path of courage, awareness, intellect, and heart.

CHAPTER FOURTEEN

Looking Forward:
Your Vision of Leadership

The real trick in life is to turn hindsight into foresight that reveals insight.

—Robin Sharma, Canadian author
and leadership speaker

Motivation to move toward a better future comes from the primal need to avoid past pain as well as from a compelling desire to achieve an improved destiny. Both are required to create lasting change. Past chapters have focused on examining your previous experiences to uncover the beliefs that have created dissatisfaction with your leadership. This has helped solidify your motivation for change. You know what aspects of your superpower you want to maintain and which parts you want to discard. Now it is time to shift from avoiding pain to achieving happiness. This final step helps you define the leader you yearn to be from a positive vantage point. When you create an incredibly clear image of what you desire, you can't help but achieve it.

Without this optimistic vision of your future, your change efforts will be based on fear. When anxiety dictates action, you edit your behavioral responses based on what you don't want to be rather than what you want to be. You attempt to avoid what you learned to dread: being seen as weak, lazy, stupid, not good enough, arrogant, careless, selfish, heartless, or whatever fear rings true for you. This angst-driven motivation confines the leader to a goal of containing the undesired behavior in order to avoid the pain of embarrassment, guilt, or shame resulting from overreacting to perceived threats. Although powerful, acting from fear is not positive to overall health. It requires being in a constant state of vigilance for triggers, stressors, and slips. This heightened fight-or-flight alertness leads to physical exhaustion. When the leader is exhausted, he is more prone to missing potential emotional triggers and overreacting to a perceived threat on his self-concept. Add this to dealing with the normal stressors of work, and a vicious cycle is created with the leader becoming even more exhausted, trying harder to be on guard, and making more mistakes. Finally, the frustrated leader abandons hope and resorts to believing his leadership is unchangeable.

There is, however, a fairly simple solution to create a positive catalyst for change—joy. Joy is a very powerful emotion and the antithesis of fear. Joy implies pleasure, happiness, confidence, contentment, bliss, and delight. It is something to run toward, not away from. Fear creates a picture of what you want to avoid, while joy creates an energizing blueprint of what you want to achieve. Joy does not trigger the flight-or-fight response. It does not keep the body and adrenal glands in a constant state of panic.

Both fear and joy can be used to create a future vision and charge forward, but the power of joy must outweigh fear to drive you toward lasting change without exhaustion. In chapter 1, I shared how Andy Grove's fear based on his past experience escaping war-torn Hungary drove him to constantly look over his shoulder. His dread of the enemy catching up to him resulted in him continually monitoring the environment for threats as he fled to safety. These same survival behaviors were triggered by the high stress of the changing landscape of the semiconductor and dot-com industry in the mid-1990s. Instead of his usually energizing vision of growth, Andy's superpower of critical evaluator became overused, and he preached his survival belief of "only the paranoid survive" throughout Intel. He constantly reminded his team that they must find the next big innovation to keep from being bested by the competition. The company shifted from a mind-set of thriving to a mind-set of surviving. Looking over shoulders and worrying about the enemy was completely exhausting. Although staff were asked to find the next big innovation, it was near impossible to be creative when the executives were finding holes in every proposal and second-guessing every move. It was difficult to take risks when the aim was perfection. Investment decisions shifted from growing capability to purchasing small start-ups that might disrupt the industry. The vision morphed from images of growth to defending the company's stronghold as number one in the industry. The company lost its energy and its source of pride.

In contrast, the earlier years at Intel were based on joy. There was less stress, Andy's past was tucked safely away, and his focus was on creation, continuous improvement, and celebration of accomplishments. The semiconductor industry was new, and the competition was less defined. Each progressive success built confidence and elation that Intel was a formidable player capable of great things. The media was touting Andy Grove as a great visionary leader, and his dream of every person in the world having access to a computer powered by Intel was exciting, compelling, and addictive. Employees had the extra energy to work sixty hours per week to reach the next objective.

Granted, things were bound to change when Intel came into the limelight years later. Intel was the Fortune 500 power player and the closely monitored bellwether stock. Excellence was a baseline expectation. A technology breakthrough in the past would have garnered a fifteen-point increase in Intel's stock, but now a similar innovation produced a single point. The competition was well defined and created an easy comparison of strengths and weaknesses. This second-guessing of every move from the market triggered Andy's survival brain, and I'm guessing he spent many nights hyperventilating over steering his massive ship through turbulent waters. Without consciously realizing that his survival beliefs were being triggered, Andy Grove unleashed his superpowers to try to save the day. He was in a defensive fight response. Without the balance of an optimistic vision, his intensity was too strong. If he had challenged this deeply programmed belief, and if he had based his vision on possibility and joy instead of staying number one, it would have changed his responses to the stressors and the company's direction. He could have balanced looking over his shoulder with looking ahead to a great future. Strategies for growth would be balanced with contingency plans for possible threats. Strategies would focus on enhancing the competitive position rather than merely fortifying past gains from future attack. The direction would have shifted from what to avoid to what to achieve. He would have been able to maintain a calmer disposition rather than being hypercritical. The unstoppable, can-do attitude that was the source of pride for the company would not have been lost during this phase of the organizational life cycle.

With your new awareness, you will be able to recognize when your leadership gets off course. Your recognition of the potential overuse of your superpowers plus your awareness of survival beliefs resurfacing will enable you to recognize when your leadership is at risk. However, if your vision of your future leadership is based on avoidance, fear, or paranoia, you will be constantly looking back over your shoulder at your interactions to criticize and berate yourself. This next step of identifying your most optimistic, joyous view of the future will keep you from acting from avoidance and instead guide you in the desired direction. Creating a positive, energizing picture of your leadership will connect to your new ways of thinking and being.

Set aside any concerns that you are not visionary, because you are. You unconsciously create mini visions of your future all the time. You daydream you are on vacation, relaxed, and enjoying your favorite activity. A smile creeps across your face as you picture the scene. You set it aside and return to focusing on work. Days later, the images pop into your head again. This time the details become more specific and more enticing. A bit later, you think of that same crystal-clear imagery, and the next minute you are blocking your calendar, buying your airline tickets, and packing for the trip. The picture you had in your mind's eye was so compelling that you couldn't help but make it happen. That is the power of a positive, joyful vision.

Creating the imagery for your best leadership is very similar. For this exploration, you will once again pay attention to your body's physical response to know when you are headed in the right direction. Think of a past vacation or another experience that brings you joy. Picture it clearly. Recall the objects, the sounds, the skin sensations from the environment, and the smells. See the people with you, and replay your carefree interactions. Notice your physical response. The muscles of the arms and legs relax, the chest expands and lifts as you take in deeper breaths, the heart slows, and a smile unconsciously spreads across your face. That smile stimulates the brain's pleasure centers, and neurotransmitters of dopamine, endorphins, and serotonin flood your system. These chemical reactions reinforce your feelings of joy and euphoria. Your brain is happy to relive the event and does not try to protect you from the memory. It wants to experience more situations that will replicate this chemical and emotional response. That's the physical response you want to become consciously aware of as you create your vision of personal leadership. These feelings put you in a state of relaxation, allowing the higher-thinking areas of your brain to remain in charge. You are creative, open to other people's ideas and critiques, and able to weigh the consequences of alternative actions and make better decisions. This is the perfect state to be in to scope your new leadership. It's expansive rather than limited. It's carefree rather than worried. In this state, you can create your best self.

Think about one of your best leadership moments—a time when you felt you were exhibiting exactly what you wanted as a leader. Feel the joy that was present at that moment. Identify the sights, sounds, and interactions that created this joy. Feel yourself expanding and becoming lighter.

Now that you are lighter, picture what your leadership will look like when it is congruent with your new beliefs. Assume it has already happened. See how you interact with others. See how you engage your team, work with your peers, collaborate with your stakeholders, and converse with the executive team and board of directors. Connect to your emotions as you experience these images. Do you feel joyful, confident, grateful, connected, contented, authentic, blissful, peaceful, or giddy? Whatever the emotion is—label it. Emotions are more powerful than content at driving behavior. Neuroscientists have proven this fact. They found that we unconsciously make decisions based on emotion and then quickly justify our choice using logic. Emotions become a powerful magnet to draw you toward your optimum leadership.

Next, visualize specific positive results from your new leadership. This is your personal change, so think in terms of how the change in interactions benefits you as well as the company. Write statements that capture these emotions, images, and benefits. (There is a worksheet to assist you with this at www.theinsightfulleader.com/book-bonuses.)

Here is an example from a leader with the visionary superpower who reprogrammed his overly ambitious time frames to create change: "I am relaxed as I align my project schedules with the slower pace of the organization because it gives me more time to ensure my team and I don't suffer burnout and to address the needs of others affected by our change." Here is an example from a results-oriented leader: "I am absolutely giddy as I recognize the few projects that require extra effort and the many tasks that I need only complete on time and within expectations. My team's workload is matched to our resources, our work hours are sane, and we maintain our energy levels."

Notice that each of the examples creates a positive image. You may need to reword your declarations to ensure you don't wander back into fear and avoidance thinking. Also, make sure that your statements are about yourself, not others. For example, the results-oriented leader originally wrote, "I am grateful I am no longer accepting every request thrown at my team, acquiescing to pressures to work long hours, and suffering burnout." This statement is both aimed at avoidance of the survival belief and makes other people's behavior the subject rather than her own. Even though it says she is no longer doing these things, it still creates a negative image, and it's easy to feel the frustration and exhaustion. This is like me saying to you, "Don't picture a German shepherd crouched in an attack position, staring at you, snarling, and foaming at the mouth" and then wondering why you don't have a picture in your mind of a happy, tail-wagging German shepherd who is excited to greet you. Again, you can feel the difference in your physical response to these two very different statements.

Continue brainstorming your statements and the enticing behaviors that elicit joy and confidence. When you feel you have no others to add, review your list, and select the five that resonate most deeply. To the beginning of each of these statements, add "Each and every day . . . " For example, "Each and every day, I am grateful to seek and accept help from others and recognize that it reduces my stress, communicates trust, and frees me to broaden my impact to the company." Edit the statements as needed to make them energizing and compelling. Write or type these five statements and post them somewhere where you can check on your progress every day: an index card on your bedroom nightstand, a wallpaper on your cellphone, a piece of paper hanging in your workspace, or whatever works for you.

At the end of each day for the next four weeks, think back over your daily interactions and find ways in which these five statements were true for you. Don't limit yourself to work examples, and don't worry about achieving every aspect of your statement, especially during the first weeks. Notice how these examples connect to the feelings you identified in your statements. Feel the physical response, and allow it to soak in so it reinforces those same actions in the future. Notice how your new leadership is better serving you, your direct reports, your boss, and the company. Notice the impact it is having at home and with friends. Let that smile wash over your face; it's addictive. For the following two months, make certain that you revisit your list a minimum of every two to three days. Keep reinforcing the emotions and behaviors.

This may sound like the road to change is fairly smooth, but there will be some bumps along the way. This transition is going to be a bit like learning to drive a car. You have the knowledge, and you can envision yourself safely speeding down the road, but you're going to be a better driver of your behaviors as you practice. In the beginning, you are much more prone to accidental mishaps. Your brain isn't quite used to shifting gears from the midbrain to the higher functions when a perceived threat arises. As you increase your awareness, you will steadily become a much better operator of your mind until the new patterns of behavior become the norm. Soon your new behaviors will become second nature. It will be similar to unconsciously scanning the road ahead while you're driving, listening to the radio, and sipping a drink—all without running onto the shoulder. Knowing the predictable stages of behavioral change will help you stay alert to potential hazards during these phases of increased proficiency.

Stage 1: Retrospective Awareness

In the beginning, there will be a time when your Hulk-like behavior slips out during a stressful exchange. You will either notice it during the event or afterward. The awareness brings a heavy sigh and the thought, "Dang, I did it again."

Don't start flogging yourself. This first stage is normal. Instead, notice how you did not justify your behavior. If you have not already apologized during the encounter, do so as soon as possible. Keep the apology simple and without any pride-saving rationalization. This is not the time to add that the rationale you provided during the heated exchange is still valid.

Take a few minutes after the encounter to identify the judgments in your survival self-talk during the incident. Use this to decipher which beliefs were driving the behavior. If it isn't readily apparent, revisit your brainstormed list and find the connection. Examine the causal factors that were present that made you feel unsafe. Determine if you need to program any new conditional "if this, then that" statements to avoid a similar outcome in the future. Determine if you need to clarify your vision of success.

Remember that no one is privy to your self-analysis, so be brutally honest about your judgments. Don't expect that you won't still think of them in this first phase. Those thoughts of "You've got to be kidding! Are they that stupid? Can't they do/see/be (insert judgment here)?" are normal. They are also perfect for determining which of your superpowers you need to examine.

Here is one of mine. "You've got to be kidding! Are they that stupid? Can't they see that they are missing the bigger picture? They are so busy fretting over the here and now that they are going to crater our organization. It's a wonder we aren't ripe for a buyout!"

Notice my use of the word "see" and the comparison of the "here and now" to the "bigger picture." This was obviously my visionary superpower causing all sorts of havoc in the heat of the moment. My survival belief it was tied to was "picture a better tomorrow and chart a course to get there." I viewed the group's lengthy discussion of the current problems as being pessimistic and providing excuses as to why we wouldn't be able to reach our vision. That elicited fear and anxiety that they were not committed to the vision. I had helped set the future direction, so I unconsciously interpreted their remarks as a personal attack. Intellectually, I knew this wasn't the case, but my survival brain was triggered. I had not yet determined a causal statement to deal with this situation. Using more rational thought, I set a new conditional statement: "If there is disagreement or concern about a step in the plan to the future, then it doesn't mean the individual or group is contesting the overall plan or final destination." With this new programming, the next time a criticism was raised, I saw it for what it was—a debate about the merits of one smaller aspect of the plan. Instead of my mind chatter going off, I actually listened to the points being made.

While I was processing through this reprogramming, I smiled at the irony of my previous thinking. Notice how my judgment insinuated that those in the meeting should have been more like me. My conviction of their stupidity and inability to see the big picture were just assumptions that my gifts and dysfunctions were somehow better than theirs. I was also inferring that they should have had the exact same life-and-death concern over plotting a course to a better future as I had.

Recognizing that I did not need to take myself so seriously was proof that I was starting to let go of my defenses. I was loosening my hardwired beliefs from absolute doctrines to theories that required examination. As you move through this first stage, approach yourself with curiosity, humor, and awareness of your human fallibility.

Stage 2: Judging But Not Acting

This deeper awareness to be on the lookout for your superpower enables you to move into the next phase of personal change. You are more aware of your emotional judgments as they are happening. In this stage, if someone says something that triggers negative judgments about the person or situation, you are consciously aware that this is your defensive mind chatter. You begin to react but then catch yourself midsentence. You take a deep breath, connect back to your personal vision, and quickly redirect your comment. Afterward, you think, "Whoa, where did that thought come from?" This is the perfect question to ask. Your frontal lobe is already proving that it is engaged. This inquiry doesn't need to be answered right away. Instead, it can easily be set aside so you can continue to focus on the discussion in the room. After the meeting, use that curiosity to find out what triggered the critical evaluation of others. You'll quickly locate the belief. It will also be easier to see the faulty, absolute thinking behind the belief. You will find yourself smiling at the recognition that you almost reacted but instead have proof that you are changing.

In this stage, it is important you find the right balance of using your superpower. Be careful of overcorrection. There can be a tendency to censor unnecessarily. Remember, the organization wants your abilities. They need your gifts. If you get the feeling that you are biting your tongue or holding in a response, examine your self-talk. Changing behavior doesn't mean not speaking up when there are valid reasons for sharing your opinion. The intensity of your response is your cue to determine if you are balanced and on track to your personal vision of change. When you choose to speak in this stage, your comments will be rational and void of self-protection.

Stage 3: A Calmer Mind

After several weeks, you will notice that you are no longer addicted to old beliefs. When you consciously review the month's interactions, you can identify a few events that in the past would have resulted in your brain chatter producing a barrage of biting comments, but you did not take the bait. It's time to celebrate that you have successfully shifted the old belief and are becoming the insightful leader you envisioned.

One of the best tests to determine if you have truly changed your beliefs is to monitor your behavior not only at work but also at home. It is easy to let your guard down and fall into old habits once you walk through the front door of your own space. Your energy is depleted from a day of playing nicely with others, effectively dealing with office politics, and squashing emotions to prove your leadership maturity. Once you arrive home, there is an unstated assumption that your partner, children, parents, or siblings have to accept your faults as well as your virtues. There is increased opportunity and risk to respond more intensely since you are more emotionally tied to these individuals than to work colleagues. When you start seeing major changes in the way you interact at home, you know you have reprogrammed your beliefs at a very deep level.

As you gain confidence in your new behaviors and beliefs, don't expect others to notice this stage as quickly as you do. Both at work and at home, the people you interact with aren't sure they can trust the new you yet. It will take others another three to six weeks to notice that you've changed. When they do, they may not be able to pinpoint exactly what has transformed. You may receive generalized positive comments, such as that you appear less stressed. Others may notice the difference but worry that they or the company will lose the advantage of your superpower's edge. These people may say you seem detached or less engaged. Don't let this bother you. They are just adjusting to the calmer you. It's natural for others to think something is wrong with someone when his energy dramatically shifts. Give it a few more weeks and they will become more comfortable with the change and appreciate the results.

Because of this delay in receiving recognition for your hard work, it is important to take time to acknowledge your journey. Stop and reminisce about where you started. Smile and feel pride for each step you accomplished. Continue to revisit your vision statements and identify ways in which you have modeled the behaviors and have experienced the feelings of joy. Celebrate the major milestones as well as the steps in the right direction toward your journey of change. It's too easy to focus on the small misses or the gaps to your ideal self. Every one of the superpowers has a bit of perfectionism entangled with it. Be wary of the tendency to evaluate your leadership against someone else's image of a perfect leader. It only takes a quick look through the magnitude of blogs, articles, and books with titles such as "The Ten Things Great Leaders Do," "Twenty Ways to Be the Ultimate Leader," or "How to Emulate the Greatest Leaders Who Ever Lived," to recognize that it would be impossible to do everything suggested. It's impractical to live up to everyone's standards. Leaders are human, and humans are fallible. Don't try to meet your employees' grandiose expectations of a great leader either. They are reading the same blogs. Of course they are going to complain when you aren't perfect. To be faultless, you would need to possess every strength of every superpower. By now, you know you can't possibly have all these gifts. Imagine the constant barrage of survival thinking you would have had to experience in order to acquire them. Nor would you want to monitor each for overuse. Be thankful this is not the case. Instead, continue to hold yourself accountable to your five positive vision statements and celebrate your continued success.

CHAPTER FIFTEEN

Looking Up: Moving to a Higher Level of Leadership

She made broken look beautiful and strong look invincible. She walked with the Universe on her shoulders and made it look like a pair of wings.

—Ariana Dancu, Canadian poet and writer

Once you're feeling confident that you are an insightful leader, you may start thinking about expanding your leadership career. Others notice your new self-awareness, increased patience, improvement in coaching your team, better interpersonal interactions, and, of course, your positive superpowers. Because the balance of IQ and EQ is so highly sought, it's only natural that your name will come up as a candidate for higher-visibility projects, succession planning, and promotion. You may or may not be aware of their interest, so if expanding your influence is something you desire, there are some things worth knowing that relate to your journey.

Changing Resistant Perceptions

Sometimes a past reputation continues to haunt a leader's career even after the person has changed. It may seem unfair, but think of it from the viewpoint of others. For a long period of time, the leader was known as being critical, unemotional, a know-it-all, condescending, unrealistic, or whatever label defined the superpower's overuse. The leader's hot buttons were known. Others could predict when the leader was going to get angry, defensive, or combative. This consistency and predictability led to trust—not the kind of trust a leader wants from others, but trust nonetheless. Imagine finally figuring out the rules to deal with a difficult or toxic leader at work and all of a sudden the rules no longer apply. That can be unsettling or even scary. Others don't want to wrongly assume the leader's new behaviors are permanent only to have their heads bitten off the following week. Luckily, direct reports and colleagues will be able to accept their leader's transformation in a matter of two to three months once they have accumulated enough positive experiences to once again predict the leader's responses.

However, it is often the more senior leaders who are resistant to acknowledge a leader's evolution. Since they rarely engage with the leader for long periods of time, they rely on stories of encounters from others. Unfortunately, many times they are relying on old data. I encountered this numerous times while facilitating succession planning and promotional discussions. While debating a leader's suitability and readiness for advancement, one executive would provide a vivid anecdote indicative of the leader's past amplified superpower. Others would join in the storytelling, speaking as if the events were currently happening. I would stop the conversation and ask for dates on the examples provided. The stories were usually secondhand accounts that took place years ago. When I asked for any examples within the last six months, the question would be met by silence. I'd inquire if there were any contrary instances within the last six months. Slowly an example would be provided and then another would follow until soon there was an overwhelming amount of data proving the leader's change. Although the selection team member acknowledged the leader's growth, sometimes there was still reluctance to promote the leader or list the person as a successor. It required challenging the group to define a time line for when old behaviors would no longer count against an individual who had proven his openness to feedback, self-reflection, and change. This was the jolt of reality needed to get the selection team member to drop the legacy.

To ensure that your history isn't affecting your future, find one or two leaders in key positions who have directly witnessed your change to serve as your champions. Ask them to speak up and support you if others make assumptions based on past experience rather than on current data. When names are being vetted for succession planning, promotion, high-visibility projects, or coveted assignments, you need someone present who will speak on your behalf. If you don't see evidence that perceptions about you are changing, ask your champions if there are other behaviors standing in your way of success. You may find some insight into the next superpower to improve.

An Increase in Candid Feedback

Once your primary superpower has been brought into balance, you may start to notice that your secondary superpower becomes more apparent to others. It's not that this superpower has increased its amplification to fill the void of the first. Instead, others now know you are open to people's perspectives and trust you will act on this feedback. This makes it easier for someone to approach you earlier when he or she sees a somewhat counterproductive behavior. This unsolicited feedback is a positive sign, so don't mistakenly interpret this as meaning you're still not good enough. Observers of your initial superpower waited until the pain of interacting with you outweighed the risk of speaking out because they feared you would become defensive or combative or verbally attack them. With your proven change, they see you are less defensive. They trust they can tell you earlier and with less frustration. Take this as a positive sign that others now see you as an insightful leader.

The great news with this early feedback is that you are immediately open to finding the connected superpower and challenging your beliefs. You can skip the first part of this book and jump right into linking the feedback to a superpower. You will find you are able to work through the steps for your second superpower at a quicker pace, since you know how to quiet your natural defenses.

Monitoring Your Energy

Being asked to solve more mission-critical issues, lead more cross-functional or organization-wide teams, and take on more responsibility is proof that you have increased your value. It feels great to be asked to expand your impact on the company. Just be aware of how all this added responsibility is affecting your energy so that you don't spread yourself too thin, begin to show signs of stress, and encounter a surprising return to less-than-effective behaviors. This is the time to consider if all the reinforcement is unintentionally shifting your energy. If it is, consider options to get back to an energy level that allows you to stay an insightful leader. Here are a few ways to regain your energy:

- *Schedule a strategic day.* Block out a day to get away from the constant flow of meetings and projects to raise your perspective to more strategic matters. This will help you decide what is most important to focus on and to course correct where you and your team have gotten pulled into tasks that are nice-to-dos rather than need-to-dos.

- *Communicate priorities.* Get agreement from your boss and stakeholders on the priorities of your workload. Often others put pressure on you based on their limited view of everything you are trying to juggle. If you can't drop one of your responsibilities, negotiate where you need more time, more resources, or more money in order to achieve all the requests in their priority order.

- *Find an adrenal release.* Carve out sacred time to release the flight-or-fight responses that accumulate from the normal stressors of work and home. Whether this is exercise, yoga, meditation, playing with the kids, or some other activity that reenergizes you, make certain that your work schedule does not become so overloaded that you find this time being eaten away.

Deciding It Is Time for a Change

If you find that you are not getting the opportunities you desire, you may feel it is time to make a different kind of change. You may decide it is time to update your résumé and find a fresh start with a different part of the organization or with a new company. Be careful not to come to this conclusion prematurely. Make certain that you have actually proven to yourself and others that your superpower is balanced. Too often a leader who hasn't completed the deeper belief and vision work is still focused on containing the behavior. She insists her future will be better with a new boss, new colleagues, or a different company culture. Somehow everything will be perfect if the players change. As you continue working on yourself, you will start to notice that, surprisingly, others you interact with seem more positive, your peers aren't as irritating, and the job or company seems like a better fit. It may appear that others around you are changing for the better; however, it is actually your energy that is shifting. Because there is no longer an undercurrent of fear, your interactions are more positive, and others want to listen to what you have to say. Interestingly, it is you who has changed, and others are reflecting that positive transformation. Before you conclude that it's time to uproot your career, make certain you give yourself sufficient opportunity to improve yourself. If afterward you decide it's time to move on, you will be able to have your fresh start with the confidence of knowing how to bring the gifts of your superpowers to the new company.

Acknowledging You Are More Than Good Enough

Remember that there is an aspect of perfectionism to each of the superpowers. No one is perfect, so learn to be less self-critical. Recognize that every leader, every executive, every person has his own survival programming. Yours is no worse or better. There will be times when a belief hidden in your unconscious surfaces. This does not mean you have not changed. Your advantage is that you are now much more attuned to noticing when you are off the course to your vision of your best leadership. You have the tools to challenge your superpowers, your programming, and your beliefs. You are able to quickly course correct and continue to learn and grow. Remember to look at these new insights with humor and as proof of how far you have come on your journey.

Stand proudly in your strengths and contributions. They are uniquely yours and are gifts to the organization. No one else experienced your past. No one else brings your exceptional perspective. No one else spent decades perfecting those exact abilities.

Likewise, recognize your evolution and the difference your presence brings. You serve as a role model to others. Your insights make you a better coach to your team. You may even be surprised to find someone coming to you for advice on how to gain a strength you would have previously seen as a gap.

Most of all, acknowledge that you are an insightful leader.

A Few Final Reminders

It is too easy to look back at the misses you made in the past. History is a good teacher but an ineffective motivator. You cannot change the past. Forget regret. Instead, stay focused on the present and consider what you can do right now to be your best self.

Don't worry if you stumble along the way because it is bound to happen. Leadership is a place where you are surrounded by hundreds of interactions, each one like a mirror pointed at you. The greater your scope of responsibility, the more magnified each blemish becomes. The good news is that your team, your peers, and those above you are willing to forgive you when you falter as long as you are willing to put the work into polishing your edges.

After I had spent months aspiring to become a friendlier and more compassionate leader, I nervously gathered my team together to ask for feedback on improvements they had seen. They were positively giddy as they gushed with examples. I was feeling very proud until one brave soul added, "We knew you could do it, Carlann, because we were praying for you." The team smiled broadly and nodded in unison. This was not some figure of speech. They all went to church every Sunday and were literally praying for me. That is how much I was affecting their lives. This is how much leaders affect the health of the organization. Don't make your team pray for you, and don't beat yourself up for not being perfect. Leadership is a constant journey of self-improvement. After any stumble, become the neutral observer, and uncover your superpowers and limiting beliefs. Do your deepest work now so your rough edges only need minor polishing later.

As you continue your journey, remember the following:

- Be grateful for your past, for it gave you your superpower and made you the leader you are today.
- Be thankful for your present, because you are releasing past fears and finding greater joy in work and life.
- Be excited about your future, because you are confidently moving in the direction of your dreams.
- Be gracious to others who have not yet started on their own journey of change.

You can find other ways to continue your work and share your success at www.theinsightfulleader.com.

Index

Abundance mentality, 12

Adrenaline, 8, 18, 114, 144; adrenal release, 156

Adversity: analytical thinking and, 43, 44, 76; anxiety and, 32; appreciating the past, 140–141; beliefs and, 133–134, 136–137; emotional intelligence and, 54; empathy and, 60; exaggerated expectations and, 38; finding one's adversity, 13, 125, 128–132; humbleness and, 92; insightful leadership and, 125, 128–134, 136–137, 140–141; preciseness and, 96; rising from adversity, 3–13; visionary thinking and, 71

Analytic thinking. *See* Highly analytic superpower

Angelou, Maya, 123

Aniston, Jennifer, 57

Anxiety, 4; adversity and, 32, 129; beliefs and, 74; calm under pressure superpower and, 113, 114, 118, 119, 120; deep breathing and, 28; flight-or-fight response and, 19; insightful leadership and, 143, 149; risk-aversion and, 12; visionary superpower and, 71, 73, 74

Apathetic perception of calm under pressure superpower, 16, 114–120

Appreciation: for bosses, 37; expressing, 43, 77, 79, 80, 82, 83, 94, 101, 117, 120; for family, 43, 46; for oneself, 65; for the past, 125, 132, 139–141; perceived as patronizing, 88; for superpowers, 24, 27, 60, 67, 70, 71, 73, 86–87, 95, 98, 114. *See also* Gratitude

Awareness, 11, 17, 20, 25; retrospective awareness, 149–150; self-awareness, 53, 81, 124–125 128, 134, 140–141, 145, 147–150, 153; social awareness, 52

Beliefs, 4–6: analytic thinking and, 76; anxiety and, 74; calm mind and, 118, 151; candid feedback and, 155; challenging beliefs, 11, 13, 16, 44, 118, 135–136, 155; defensiveness and, 19, 20; egalitarianism and, 87, 89, 90; emotions and, 65, 74, 77, 83; identifying beliefs, 4, 13, 133–135; insightful leadership and, 125, 128–141, 144–145, 147, 149–151, 155–158; judging but not acting

About the Author

Carlann Fergusson is an award-winning leadership-change expert, past corporate executive, speaker, and founder of Propel Forward. She guides experienced leaders in becoming more insightful and strategic. Although a psychologist by education, she discovered her coaching and consulting methods while rising through the ranks of corporate leadership at Intel, Visteon, Press Ganey, and Meijer. In addition to assisting a variety of corporate and individual clients, Fergusson serves on the adjunct faculty for Northwestern University's Leadership Certificate Program in Chicago. Her expertise has been cited in *CBS MoneyWatch, International Business Times, Newsday,* and *The Boston Globe.*